MIGHTIER THAN THE SWORD

Mightier than the Sword

MARY WHITEHOUSE

KINGSWAY PUBLICATIONS

EASTBOURNE

ISBN 0 86065 382 X

Biblical quotations are from the
Authorized Version (crown copyright).

Cover design by Vic Mitchell

Printed in Great Britain for
KINGSWAY PUBLICATIONS LTD
Lottbridge Drove, Eastbourne, E. Sussex BN23 6NT by
Cox & Wyman Ltd, Reading.
Typeset by Nuprint Services Ltd, Harpenden, Herts.

Beneath the rule of men
    entirely great
The pen is mightier than
    the sword

Richelieu
by Lord Edward Lytton

Contents

Foreword		9
Introduction		11
1	A Long Way from John Wesley	20
2	Where Our Caravan Rested	36
3	Children at Risk	46
4	Censorship—A Wicked Word	57
5	'None So Blind…'	79
6	'There Can Be No Defence…'	89
7	'Just a Matter of Taste?'	100
8	The Schoolmaster in the Lions' Den	110
	Conclusion	120
	Epilogue: 'Go to It, Girl!'	124

Appendices

1	The British Humanist Association	130
2	BBC and ITV telephone numbers and addresses	133
3	Video Recordings Act	136
4	The NVALA's comments upon The Home Office Committee on Obscenity and Film Censorship	137

5 Local Government (Miscellaneous
  Provisions) Act 1982   139
6 Monitoring   142
7 Paedophile Information Exchange   152
8 The Post Office Act, 1953   154
9 Information and Advice on Objecting to
  the Granting of Sex Shop Licences   155
10 The Beliefs and Aims of National VALA   158

Foreword

From any point of view Mary Whitehouse is unique in our time.

But I have no doubt that history will give her a place amongst that select band of men and women who in the name of Christ have done so much for so many. What Wilberforce, Shaftesbury, Fry, Booth and Barnado were to their day, Mary is to the television age. Each of these believed with Edmund Burke that 'All that is necessary for evil to flourish, is for good men to do nothing' and each of them achieved so much because they went into battle, not in their own strength, but in the strength of Christ.

Throughout the eight years during which I have been privileged to work closely with Mary, I have found myself asking time and time again how it is that she is able to retain her equanimity in the face of oceans of apathy. How is it she retains her extraordinary serenity when pounded by rolling breakers of hostility? How does she keep her 'saltiness' in the face of such rotten-ness all around? How is it that she is not overwhelmed by the darkness she seeks to combat? What has enabled her to be so single-minded in pursuing her goal? What vision or motivation keeps a woman of 75 years as active and determined as only a very few are in the prime of life?

The answer to all these questions is of course Mary's simple but profound Christian faith. She does not wear that faith on her sleeve because she has not been called to preach. Whenever she speaks in public she does not deviate from her goal of seeking to expose the evils which threaten to overwhelm our society. But behind every engagement there is a preparation of prayer and dependence upon her Lord.

So I, for one, am delighted that she has been persuaded to write this book. Such a person must have a wealth of devotional gems in the spiritual bank and all of us who read this book will be the richer for being privileged to share them.

John J. Smyth, Q.C.

Introduction

The word of the Lord came to me: 'Son of man, speak to your countrymen and say to them: "When I bring the sword against a land and the people of the land choose one of their men and make him their watchman, and he sees the sword coming against the land and blows the trumpet to warn the people, then if anyone hears the trumpet but does not take warning and the sword comes and takes his life, his blood will be on his own head. Since he heard the sound of the trumpet but did not take warning, his blood will be on his own head. If he had taken warning, he would have saved himself. But if the watchman sees the sword coming and does not blow the trumpet to warn the people and the sword comes and takes the life of one of them, that man will be taken away because of his sin, but I will hold the watchman accountable for his blood."'

Ezek 33:1–6

I find myself quoting these words with some diffidence. It might seem that I give myself some *special* place. But that is not so. We are *all* 'sons of men'—we are all called to 'blow the trumpet', and we shall all be held 'accountable' if we do not.

I do not know how many more years the Lord will give me to fight the battle (how else can I describe it?)

which has filled my life for the last twenty-one years. What I do know is that the work must go on.

Many times people have asked me: 'Who will take over the work of National VALA when you can no longer lead it?' I have always had to answer, 'I do not know!' Not because I have been unwilling to know, far from it; nor because there is a shortage of people who could most effectively take over. There are two reasons. Firstly, I have always had a deep sense that 'the work is the Lord's' and that he will make his purpose clear in his own time. Secondly, I have increasingly realized that with the passing of the years the nature of the work would change and would continue to change, as indeed it is bound to do if it is genuinely 'free' and not tied to human ambition or preconditions. In that situation quite a different sort of person might well be called for.

But time *does* pass, and one comes to realize that the privilege and (to be honest) the burden need to be carried by more and more people. Indeed I would go so far as to say 'by everyone who cares'—that, I imagine, means just about all of us!

Although we did not realize, in the early days, how much the Press prefers to focus on an individual rather than on a movement, we came to accept this not only as a fact of public life but also as a challenge. But the claim that I and my immediate friends and colleagues were no more than 'a voice crying in the wilderness' with little support in the country as a whole was never true. Far from it! The first petition we ever launched ('Clean Up TV' in January 1964, when we were a small handful of people with no organization behind us) collected half a million signatures in four months instead of the 30-40,000 we had hoped for. This fact alone gives some indication of the widespread anxiety which focused on the activities of the BBC (particularly) at that time.

Since when, while it is true that the great tide of public support which flowed during those early months and years was slowed down by the organized counter-attack launched by the humanist/permissive lobby inside and outside broadcasting, the ground swell of public concern has continued to grow.

We stand now at a most critical point, not only in our social but also in our political life. The moral anarchy which has characterized the last two or three decades is now spilling over into industrial and political anarchy. The question we all have to ask ourselves at this time is not only 'What should be done?' but also 'What can *I* do?'. I hope this book will stimulate at least some of the answers.

But the matter goes far deeper than that. To put it in a nutshell: whether or not we are able and willing to make an effective and positive contribution to the great moral debates of our time depends upon in whose strength we do it. We must, I believe, fully accept that God will take us not only into unknown ways but also into unimaginable ones, if only we will let him.

The story of Peter walking on the water is never very far from my consciousness, and it holds an all-pervading challenge to me. If we move only in those circumstances and with those people of whom we have at least some knowledge and experience, then we are simply humanists—however sincere our intention. We need constantly to live beyond our depth and outside our own circle of friends. Especially we must not be limited by our natural gifts. I sometimes think that these very gifts can be a hindrance rather than a help. The more of them we have, the less we feel the need to throw ourselves upon the mercy and sustaining power of God. It is when we are sure of *ourselves* that we stand most in danger of failure—at least, in God's terms.

Those early days of the campaign are as vivid to me now as ever they were—the sleepless nights which followed some response I had made to an enquiring journalist, the horror I had of seeing my name in the newspapers—even more, the fear and anxiety which surrounded the business of 'being talked about'; especially as many of the newspapers and television producers set no limits to the misrepresentation and calumny in which they indulged. Mind you, I came to see that this had its positive side, since packed meetings have been a characteristic of our years of campaigning. I'm sure that at least some (if not many!) people came to see what this cranky woman looked like—'Bun on top of the head an' all!'

I had no training or experience in public speaking, and the state of my nerves before beginning to speak was such that my legs lost their feeling and my mind its power of conscious thought. But I came to realize that it is the Holy Spirit, and not some gift of oratory, which makes our words touch the hearts of people. There is nothing so 'flat' as the speech which has been delivered over and over again. And it is that prayer at the moment of emptiness before one stands up to speak, which makes the words flow with freshness and conviction.

So often the accusation of being 'negative' is thrown at those who fight against the moral and cultural anarchy of our times. When it comes my way I take comfort from the story of Nehemiah and the vision he had of a new Jerusalem (the foundations of the city had been destroyed seventy years before and had to be relaid before the city itself could be rebuilt).

The very first thing that Nehemiah and his friends did was to rebuild the wall around the city. And so it is, metaphorically speaking, in our own time. Nothing will be gained and much, indeed everything, could be lost, if we individually and collectively fail to take the true measure of the calculated and continued threat to the Judeo/Christian foundation of western democracy. The Queen is 'Defender of the Faith', our law is based upon the Ten Commandments and Parliament begins each day with prayers.

At this time of crisis there is much we can learn from Nehemiah. He spared himself nothing. He and his friends faced, and refused to run away from, every kind of threat and public and private ridicule from those who were opposed to the rebuilding of the city. He set no limits to his mental, physical and spiritual commitment. He used his brains. Above all he had a vision, and he had great perception of the way in which the devil would do his best to destroy him. He was quite uninhibited by any sense of that false modesty which can so easily cloak an unwillingness to expose oneself to the full implication of what total commitment means.

He went to see the King and asked permission to rebuild the city. The King gave it to him. Nehemiah set his 'watchers' around the wall with their trumpets at the ready so that everyone would be alerted at the first sign of danger. The builders worked from the first light of dawn until the stars came out. The opposition never let up for a moment; but, wonder of wonders, the wall was completed in fifty-two days. At *that* point, I have to confess, my sense of identification with Nehemiah and his stalwart warriors disappears!

It would be foolish for me to give anyone the idea that getting involved in this fight, which inevitably touches the very essence of what people believe and fear and care about, is a bed of roses. Far from it; and certainly, speaking out of my own experience, I would have backed out of it many years ago if I hadn't known the Source of the replenishing of my strength and of the vision of what we were called upon to do. One lesson I have learnt is that the task is far and away too large to cope with in one's own strength.

Out of all the things that have happened, all the places I have visited and all the people I have met, one experience stands out above all others. It occurred at a time of great physical and mental stress, when no day seemed to go by without some crisis to be resolved. These strains were associated not only with the work but also with family affairs, not least because my husband's brother and his wife were killed in a mid-air collision over France leaving three teenage children. I had been into the office of the Press Association in Fleet Street, and as I came out I missed my footing on the steps and went flying across the pavement. Several people came to my aid and I wasn't seriously hurt, only badly shaken. I stood for some minutes against the wall to recover my breath. And as I walked on I simply felt that I had come to the end of my tether, that I could not possibly go on.

It was at that point that the Lord came to me. He said with unforgettable love, but with great clarity and challenge, 'Mary, you feel as you do because you carry the burden on your *own* shoulders instead of giving it to me. The burden is mine, not yours.' That releasing and joyful experience remains for me as vivid today as when it happened; and while I would not, and could not, claim that since then I have never felt strained or tired —that would be a nonsense—it taught me two things.

Firstly it taught me that the burden *is* the Lord's, that the forces with which we have to reckon will destroy us unless we constantly draw on his strength, acknowledging always that our minds and bodies are inadequate for the fight.

Secondly, it taught me that when we *do* put ourselves into his hands, and set no limit to what we will do and give in terms of time, energy and resources, then he leads us in the most wonderful way. He not only gives us experiences far beyond anything we could have imagined, but also 'goes before' to protect and prepare and achieve.

I think many people ask themselves the question 'How on earth did we ever get into this mess?' and then go on to wonder how we can get out of it! I know I did; and discovering the answer has taken me and those who work with me deep into the ramifications of political, personal and financial interests not only here in Britain but in many countries across the world. I am only too aware that much of the contents of this book may well prove so unpleasant and disturbing that some of its readers may be tempted to 'skip a few pages'. But may I say, with all understanding and gentleness, that if we are to make a constructive contribution to this debate then any kind of a 'passing by on the other side' will be a kind of betrayal.

Although it is twenty-one years since Norah Buckland and I began this work with the full and continuing support of our husbands, people still want to know 'How did it all begin?'

The story of Norah's experiences in her work in the parish of Longton, Staffordshire, where her husband Basil was Rector, and the story of mine in my school work have been told many times (most recently in my last book *A Most Dangerous Woman?*[1]) and I do not think it needs to be retold here. There is, however, one thing I would like to say about the origin of our campaign against the permissiveness, Godlessness, violence, sexual explicitness, crudities and general lack of responsibility—not to mention left-wing bias!—which

---

[1] *A Most Dangerous Woman?* (Lion Publishing, 1982).

characterized so much of the output of the BBC at that time. Our campaign was born out of our own personal and vivid experience of the impact of television upon the young for whom we were, in varying degrees responsible. Consequently, concern about the kind of world we are building for the young and the enormous burden we are creating for them has always been at the very heart of our work, and continues to be so. It has been in many ways a remarkable experience, to speak as I have done in the universities and in the schools during the last twenty years and to witness at first hand how the attitude of students towards what one is saying has completely changed. It has moved from almost complete hostility—which in the early years often showed itself in sometimes quite amusing (though other times unspeakable) ways—to an attitude which has resulted in a situation in which we now almost invariably win the university debates in which we participate.

One of the stories I treasure most is of a debate at Oxford University in 1981 when John Smyth, Q.C. and I debated with Victor Lownes, then head of the 'Playboy' empire in Britain. We won by a mere fifteen votes. But it was what happened afterwards that made such an unforgettable impression upon me. During the reception which followed the debate I felt a touch on my shoulder. I turned to see three very big young men— 'Rugby players!' was my first thought—behind me. 'We just wanted to tell you, Mrs Whitehouse, that we have come over from Cambridge this evening to pray for you' they said.

For Cambridge to come to Oxford—or vice versa—is as unheard of as members of the House of Lords entering the House of Commons! And we were immensely touched and grateful. So when we were invited several months later to debate with Victor Lownes again at

Cambridge we agreed and won, this time by 161 votes!

And I find it so everywhere I go—the young *do* care deeply and want something different from the kind of world we have created for them. It's up to us all to see that they are not disappointed.

And if we are to ensure that they are not, it is, I believe, essential that we are mentally as well as morally and spiritually prepared for the inevitable battle which lies ahead.

CHAPTER 1

A Long Way from John Wesley

It seems to many of us that by far the most significant feature of post-war Britain has been the retreat of Christianity and the advance of secular humanism; and that the great majority of the social, ethical, even economic problems facing us spring from this. An exaggerated statement? I don't believe so; I hope to demonstrate the truth of it, not least in the shameful failure in recent years of sections of, and sometimes the leadership of, the church, to defend and proclaim the gospel. It is failure which has permitted and facilitated the alarming success of committed humanists in spreading atheism and atheistic attitudes throughout the land, with all that that has meant to the quality of our national life.

The secularization of the West has taken place gradually over a long period of time, but the revolution which has caused the virtual collapse of Christian moral standards has happened within the last forty years. Great Britain, once a predominantly Christian country and still constitutionally a Christian country, has increasingly become, to an extent which should alarm us all, a Godless society.

The collapse of the moral structure which has characterized western society throughout its recorded history is the result of the gradual erosion of its very foundation—the Bible. This has been downgraded in the eyes of many people, from its time-honoured position as the inspired word of God to that of a collection of writings on a par with the holy books of other religions. While it is conceded that it has some limited academic interest, its message has been increasingly presented as no longer compelling and of little relevance to modern society.

For over a thousand years in this country, there was no serious challenge to the validity of the Christian ethic. Though people did wrong, few doubted that it was right, at least in principle, to be honest; that the authority of parents, schoolmasters and the law should be recognized and respected; that swearing, blasphemy, and obscenity were intrinsically wrong; that there could be no justification for vandalism and violence; that fornication and adultery were immoral, abortion evil, sodomy sinful and murder a capital offence. But all that has changed. And while there can be little doubt that compassion and understanding were often in those days conspicuous by their absence, there can also be little doubt that those two qualities alone will not bring the change that is desperately needed if our society is to be a truly caring one. The pattern of life today is little recommendation for the 'alternative society' we have created and made commonplace.

Fiddling the tax man or the Social Security is excused as a justifiable economic readjustment. Stealing from one's place of employment is regarded by too many people as a 'perk' that goes with the job. Vicious physical attacks on elderly people are commonplace. Rape is becoming accepted as just one of those things that is bound to happen from time to time however deep the shock to the person concerned. How many times are offences from theft to murder committed by people who are, defence counsel will claim, basically good, but who acted 'completely out of character', or 'under extreme provocation' and should be excused on that account?

Understandably enough, after the war our political leaders gave first priority to economic recovery and the people increasingly devoted themselves to the pursuit of personal prosperity in terms of money, material possessions, leisure activities and 'the affluent society' so that the 'you never had it so good' syndrome took over. But as so often happens, with affluence comes sexual permissiveness and a decline in moral standards. So the 'permissive society' and its values—or lack of them!—became the order of the day and has completely transformed our society.

There is a great and understandable temptation to people today, for Christians as well as non-Christians, to withdraw into smaller and smaller groups where they feel safe whether within family or church or club. Not because they are basically unwilling to grapple with the vast social evils which surround us but because the problems seem too great even to think about let alone tackle and solve. But the truth is—it's us or no one.

It has always been fashionable—understandably so—to lay the responsibility for the increasing decadence and Godlessness of our society upon the young. But the truth is that the 'permissive society' first took root long before they were born. I think it is quite difficult now for people to realize how all this crept up upon us without the vast majority of us being in the least aware, in spite of periodical press headlines, of what was really at stake, or indeed was intended.

In the early 1950s Canon Patey, then Dean of Liverpool Cathedral, said publicly, 'We Christians must listen to what humanists have to say. We can learn much from them.' So a lot of people did, including some church leaders, even though humanists totally reject the existence of God and ridicule the incarnation, the resurrection and the idea of life after death.

Launched by John Osborne's *Look Back in Anger* with its contempt for traditional moral values, the so-called 'liberal' philosophy of the permissives was given a considerable boost when Mr Roy Jenkins introduced a private member's Bill which developed into the now very much discredited Obscene Publications Act, and it progressed steadily in the sixties with timely help from the then Bishop of Woolwich, Dr John Robinson. His book *Honest to God* gave birth to such headlines as ' "God is dead" says Bishop!' What is more he went into the witness box to defend D. H. Lawrence's *Lady Chatterley's Lover*, a book that contained what the judge described as 'lurid' descriptions of adulterous behaviour but which, the Bishop claimed, portrayed 'in a real sense something sacred, an act of Holy Communion'. Then there was Dr Alex Comfort, described by the BBC[1] as an 'anarchist' who said that 'we may eventually come to realize that chastity is no more a virtue than malnutrition', described 'a chivalrous boy as one who takes contraceptives when he goes to meet his girl friend'[2] and who claimed that fidelity between husband and wife was 'an outdated conception and due for some radical re-thinking'.

The Reith lecturer, Professor Carstairs, then Professor of psychiatry at Edinburgh University, got enormous publicity from the press handout of one of his lectures, which contained the statement that 'Charity is more important than chastity'. Sir Hugh Greene, then Director General of the BBC, gave quite unprecedented

[1] 14th July, 1963.
[2] *Daily Mirror*, 15th June, 1963.

freedom in the sixties and early seventies to the exponents of the 'new morality' and to playwrights who projected foul language, blasphemy and excesses of violence and sex into the living-rooms of the country.

Throughout that decade and into the seventies there was a deliberate and sustained attack on the establishment and on traditional standards of morality—not least in so-called 'religious broadcasting'. Accepted values were ridiculed and every kind of authority was challenged, mainly through TV programmes such as 'The Wednesday Play' and 'That was the Week that was' which ridiculed patriotism and religion. The attack culminated in an episode of 'Till Death Do Us Part' when the Virgin Birth was blasphemously satirized. It was a startling and vicious attack on Christian belief which resulted in enormous controversy and protest—to little effect, for it was but one of many.

Very early in our campaigning life we became aware of the activities of the British Humanist Association (see Appendix 1) and the National Secular Society. Though numerically very small they have exerted an influence out of all proportion to their size, by formulating clear objectives, infiltrating influential bodies such as the Religious Education Council, and organizing a powerful parliamentary lobby.

We really had no excuse for not being aware of their aims, which were widely published in 1962. In general, these were to establish a secular society. In particular, their aims were to abolish religious education, laws restricting Sunday trade, sport and entertainment, and the existing blasphemy laws and obscenity laws; to ensure that 'the sexual rights of teenagers' were recognized; to allow homosexual activity, easier divorce, abortion on demand and euthanasia; to raise the age of criminal responsibility and to lower and then abolish the age of consent (which could open the way to legalized paedophile activity). They have been unbelievably successful not only through their persuasive propaganda in the media but in legislation too.

It's well worth recalling that the British Humanist Association tried hard but unsuccessfully for many years to have the religious provisions of the 1944 Education Act repealed. So, evidently realizing that it would need to change its tactics, it proposed in 1967 the inclusion of other religions and atheistic humanism in RE lessons, on the grounds that we are now a multi-faith society in which the majority lack any religious belief. Their ploy paid off handsomely and instead of Bible-based, Christ-centred RE lessons, children are now often given a sort of Cook's Tour of World Religions. Morning assembly, as many of us knew it, has long been under attack—and Sir Keith Joseph as Secretary of State for Education should be given as much support as we can muster in his attempts to preserve it. The days when children were taught the Ten Commandments and the Beatitudes at school are long gone in the great majority of State schools. Ask a youngster today 'Who or what are the Beatitudes?' and he'll think it's a new pop group!

In 1967 came the Sexual Offences Act, which legalized homosexual practices in certain circumstances; and worst of all, legislation to 'amend' the Infant Life Preservation Act of 1929, which opened the door to the Abortion Act of 1967 and subsequent Abortion Law Reform legislation which has resulted in the slaughter—how can we describe it otherwise?—of over two million unborn babies.

In 1969, too, came the Divorce Reform Act which has undermined the sanctity of marriage and the stability of home life and has caused untold misery to hundreds of thousands of young children whose lives have been torn apart emotionally. It is almost as though we have turned our backs upon even the possibility of the kind of personal commitment which has 'hope' and 'selflessness' —not to mention the promises of the marriage service— at its heart, in favour of the easy way out.

Local Authorities have been enabled to establish advisory sex clinics, which, using ratepayers' money, issue contraceptives to school children regardless of age, without parental knowledge or consent. One only needs to look at the figures for teenage abortion to realize the human tragedies which lie behind them. And so has come about the transformation of society from one based on the morality of the Bible and the Christian faith to the ethics of a secular society.

Harry Blamires, in his superb book *The Christian Mind*[1] had this to say about this surrender to materialistic values:

> There is no longer a Christian mind…the mind of modern man has been secularised….[It] has succumbed to the secular drift with a degree of weakness and nervelessness unmatched in Christian history. It is difficult to do justice in words to the complete loss of intellectual morals in the twentieth century.

And Malcolm Muggeridge, once an agnostic, has not minced his words about the situation in which we now find ourselves:

> Past civilisations have been destroyed by barbarians from outside, but we are doing this job ourselves. Our artists may safely be left to destroy art, our writers to destroy literature, our scholars to destroy scholarship, our moralists to destroy morality, and our clergy to destroy religion. We breed our own barbarians at the public expense in our groves of academy.

[1] SPCK 1963.

I mention all these events, not to drag up what is now well past, but to demonstrate how we come to be where we are. While the people I have mentioned except Sir Hugh Greene and, of course, Malcolm Muggeridge, are hardly remembered, their joint impact was immense because of the almost unlimited publicity they were given in the Press and on television and the way in which those who could, and would, have challenged their claims were censored off the screen.

I think we have to recognize from the start the immense power that television has exercised in the creation of the society we now have. It was Sir Hugh Greene himself who described television as 'the most powerful medium ever to affect the thinking and behaviour of people'. How true that is! Times have changed, and I think it highly unlikely that people propagating such morally destructive ideas as those quoted above would be given the same freedom of the screen today. This is so not only because those in charge of broadcasting at the BBC have now a very different interpretation of the responsibility laid upon them. It is also true because of the change in public attitudes, particularly amongst the many young people who see through the false, often dangerous, values propagated in the sixties and seventies, and now want something different for themselves and the families they hope to have.

'The party is over and the bills are coming in' said Digby Anderson writing in *The Times* December 5th 1984 under the headline 'Permissive hosts must pay the bill'. There can be no doubt that the threat posed by the disease AIDS has served to smash many of the illusions attached to the permissive society. The appearance of this dreadful disease has indeed acted as a catalyst; many of those who, against all logic (let alone morality) have defended so-called 'freedom' are now rapidly reconsidering their position and beginning to question many of the irrational dangerous assumptions upon which it was all based.

The mounting evidence of real suffering, even disaster, which is the inevitable consequence of the years of abdication of responsibility both in church and State, let alone in personal living is, thank God, shattering the complacency and self-interest which has lain at the very heart of the permissive society.

AIDS is linked with promiscuous homosexuality—and we do well to remember that the legalizing in this country of adult homosexuality was one of the first of the so-called permissive reforms. 'Permissive for whom?' one is often tempted to ask. Certainly not for those babies known to have lost their lives through transfusion of blood donated by homosexuals suffering from AIDS, even though (in all fairness) it must be said that they did not realize that they were carrying the disease.

Herpes and gonorrhoea are both connected with promiscuity. There is a likelihood that the incidences of cervical cancer in young women is connected with early sexual activity—and we must all surely be aware of the pressure from various contraception lobbies to make 'the pill' available even to the youngest of adolescent girls, not to mention the increasing problem—highlighted by recent court cases in this country and abroad—of the sexual abuse of children.

Leaving the suffering implicit in all this on one side for a moment, let us look at its cost in hard cash alone. I quote from Digby Anderson's article again: while he concedes that 'the bills' can be disputed and that the problems are complex, they are nevertheless highly disturbing, give or take something either way. He speaks of divorce running at 147,000 a year, 1,100% up on the pre-war figure and costing perhaps £1,000 million a year in legal bills, Social Security, child care and medical expense. Almost 35,000 abortions for the first quarter of 1984. Extrapolated for the year, that is 139,656 foetuses aged up to 150 days, killed at perhaps £500 each. And while in 1960 taxpayers spent £15 million on one-parent families, today we spend £1,000 million.

Digby Anderson goes on to say, 'It is now up to the progressives to defend their revolution. It can no longer be taken for granted.' He concludes that with hindsight, it is obvious that the so-called progressive reforms,

> were not founded on facts and reason but very limited information and questionable assumptions. In short, they were experiments. It is crucial that they should be reassessed. Such evidence as we now have is not sufficient to condemn them but it is enough to shift the burden of proof. It is no longer up to the sceptics to show that the permissive revolution was a mistake: it is for its increasingly beleaguered supporters to justify its continued incorporation in law and welfare provision. The bills are currently addressed to them.

It is up to us to deliver them.

And if we are to do so effectively then we do need to take time to study what has gone on either 'behind our backs' as it were, or without us being aware of the consequences of what may have seemed trivial at the time and not worth making a fuss about.

It is perhaps only now, while (we must hope) there is still time and opportunity for action, that we can trace the pattern and the purpose of the anti-God manipulators within our society.

Although the work of the National Viewers & Listeners Association (National VALA) began in 1964 as 'The Clean Up TV Campaign' it became very obvious as the years went by that simply attacking the failures of

broadcasting would never solve the pressing problems
which were so apparent within radio and television.
Time without number, indeed almost invariably, the
defence offered by the broadcasting authorities has been
that any particular offence was justified because it
'reflected the society in which we live'. The fact that
such a response indicated an abdication of the obligations[1] laid upon both authorities by Parliament and
by law to ensure as far as possible that nothing is
included in programmes 'which offends against good
taste or decency...or is likely to encourage or incite to
crime or lead to disorder...or to be offensive to public
feeling' seemed to matter little to some of those immediately involved in the production of programmes.
At the same time those ultimately responsible for their
content and quality, the Governors of the BBC and the
Independent Broadcasting Authority, seemed allergic
to any admission of failure; not least, one suspects,
because they were largely ignorant of what had happened until after the event. Then they found themselves
faced with a choice of being—in their terms—disloyal
to their staff or apparently condoning violation of the
obligations laid upon them. It was a choice made more
difficult for the BBC because the whole of the Corporation was to all intents and purposes indivisible, while
the Independent companies functioned quite independently of the IBA which was, consequently, in a position
—if its members would only take it—of making and
publishing its own assessments.

In 1983 we published a report entitled *It Makes You
Wonder Why You Bother!*—a quote from a disillusioned
viewer's letter. The report dealt with letters of complaints to the BBC and the IBA and the response

[1]Television Act 1954, Broadcasting Act 1981.

received from the Broadcasting Authorities. In the case of the BBC these varied from none at all to the assurance, in a very few instances, that the letter had been found 'invaluable'—though what value they actually proved to have been was always too difficult to discover. In reply to a complaint about bad language, for example, a viewer is assured that 'producers are constantly reminded of the need to guard against any increase in the use of bad language'; though, one can't help but wonder what notice producers take of such reminders, since the use of bad language is more prevalent now than it ever was! Another stock response makes those who have written feel that there must be something a bit odd about them; apparently 'no one else wrote to complain'.

I have been constantly reminded of how *few* people actually do pick up their pens to speak their minds. Only a few weeks before writing this I was speaking to an audience of about 600—the great majority of them committed Christians—which was obviously greatly concerned. I asked them first 'How many of you have felt offended by something you've seen on television during the last year?' and a sea of hands went up. I then asked 'How many have actually phoned or written to say so?' Only *seven* hands went up! Perhaps we've only got ourselves to blame. (Incidentally, I usually follow this up by enquiring 'How many of you wrote to thank and congratulate producers for programmes you've really enjoyed?' which is equally important. But the response to that is usually the same.)

It has to be said, of course, that the type of reply received—often no more than a card of acknowledgement—makes people feel that writing in the first place was a waste of time. And if I may make a suggestion here—it really is most important that we are specific about what has offended or pleased us. I fear that too many people write in the most general terms saying that they thought that such and such a programme was 'a disgrace and should never have been transmitted' or something to that effect. You may think that's an exaggeration but it isn't—as many of the complaints which reach us demonstrate!

It is far more effective to state precisely the name and time of transmission of the programme and which particular episode, or use of bad language, gave offence. It could also be the general tone or bias within a programme, or even the treatment—was it balanced and fair?—meted out to participants in current affairs programmes.

I know it sounds a lot of trouble, but it's very well worth it. Keep a copy of your letter! Then if you receive no reply or what you feel is a thoroughly unsatisfactory one, send both a copy of your letter and the reply to your M.P. and ask him to take up the matter with the broadcasting authority concerned. You may also find that such correspondence will give you the material for a letter to your local Press.

Perhaps I could add a further piece of advice. Our experience has shown that 'round robin' letters are nothing like as effective as single ones, though two or three signatures are fine. This is really what participation is all about—if people are prepared to sign *your* letter, they really should make the additional effort to write their own. The BBC and IBA count how many complaints they receive—a 'round robin' counts only as one! (See Appendix 2.)

And if we're tempted, as we often must be, to ask ourselves 'what's the use?' or persuade ourselves that we have far more important things to do, then I repeat that it was the former Director General of the BBC, Sir Hugh Greene, who said 'Television is the most powerful medium ever to affect the thinking and behaviour of people.' And he should know.

But because it is such a powerful and all-pervasive medium, television is bound to play a key role, for better or worse, in creating the quality of life we all experience. It therefore demands our attention and our involvement—not least, I would suggest, because a Department of Education and Science Report[1] on children's viewing habits showed that young people between the ages of five and fourteen spend an average of twenty-three hours a week watching television!

Changes in public attitudes can now come about almost overnight, whereas prior to the advent of television and indeed radio social change, for better or worse, evolved over years of academic discussion on the one hand or pressure through successive generations at the grass roots on the other. This gave time for the dross to be filtered out and cooler assessments of what was good or bad to be made. In assessing the power of television one only has to recall the lifetime it took Wilberforce to achieve legislation ending the slave trade, and how John Wesley travelled 225,000 miles on horseback and preached 50,000 sermons in towns and villages all over the country. These so affected public response to the Christian faith that the course of history in Britain was changed.

We live in a very different world! Audiences for television programmes are counted, in exceptional circumstances like Royal Weddings, in hundreds of millions of viewers. All this can be very exciting; and there is no doubt that, through television, our eyes have been opened and our understanding extended in ways which would have been quite inconceivable to people

[1] *Popular television and school* (1983).

living in pre-television days. That the TV screen has given immense comfort and pleasure to countless people there can be no doubt, and there is also no doubt that we should all say so more often than we do.

But the fact remains that, because of the very nature of television (a programme comes and goes, and we're straight into the next) its immediate impact can be very great but only rarely is there any opportunity to discuss and assess and, if need be, challenge its content—in spite of 'Points of View' which is primarily an entertainment programme (though in all fairness, credit must be given to Channel 4's 'Right to Reply' which is a much more honest and impartial programme. So much so that it received the National VALA Award for 1984!).

And in asking ourselves what sort of priority should be given to a meaningful audience participation in the maintenance and creation of broadcasting standards we have to see that question, I believe, as an integral and vital part of the immeasurable challenge created for every one of us by the whole philosophy of the so-called 'permissive society' in which everyone of us, irrespective of the depth of our commitment to the Christian faith, actually lives. We cannot wrap our clothes around ourselves and walk by on the other side, or even just look on in pity. We *have* to do something, or the generations which follow us will never forgive us. And perhaps God will not, either.

To help us on the way, let's remember that both the BBC and the IBA have a legal obligation to take viewer and listener reaction into account. The great question, of course, is how they then apply, in terms of programme standards, what they have learnt from such reaction!

As we think about the effect that television may be having upon ourselves and our children, we need also to bear in mind how potent a vehicle for change it is, not only in our society, but around the world. It is creating—for better or worse—a sort of 'world culture'. British television programmes, not least because of their technical brilliance, have a very ready market not only in, say Australia and the United States, but also in non-English speaking countries (where they are shown with sub-titles). They are even shown in under-developed countries where television, even though it might seem that the money involved could be better spent in other ways, often provides a means of escape from the difficulties and problems of everyday life.

I believe that one of the problems we face is what I call the 'switch off' syndrome. You know, 'She doesn't like it, so why doesn't she switch off'—how many countless times has one heard that! But it's a facile and indeed irresponsible attitude. Of course, it's easy to turn a knob, but that doesn't end the transmission— except for us. And if it's true, as is now clearly established, that television does have such a great, indeed immeasurable effect, then we must surely never forget that whether or not we switch off the television set, we cannot switch off from the society in which it exists and helps to create. The truth is that there is *no* way we can protect ourselves from the impact of television, nor, I think, should we want to. I may say that the Broadcasting Authorities themselves reject such a defence and do not use it, though plenty of other people do.

CHAPTER 2

Where Our Caravan Rested

One of the most vivid examples of how, when God gives
a vision of what needs to be done, he moves to ensure its
fulfilment without delay, came during the election campaign of 1983. We were increasingly concerned about
the threat, particularly to children, of the production
and distribution of what came to be known as the 'video
nasties'. When the 1983 election was called we felt that,
somehow or other, it had to be made an election issue.
We had already done much to make it a public issue
and there was considerable concern in the country.

Parliament had been dissolved and time was short
when the thought came—why not take our campaign
into as many marginal parliamentary seats as was practical in the three weeks left? To be really effective we
had to be seen and heard by as many people as possible
in those areas. But how? I was recovering from a painful
injury to one of my legs, and there was no way in which
I was going to be able to stand, let alone walk! 'How
about a caravan?' someone suggested. And in a matter
of a few days we were offered one—and what a comfort-
able and splendid vehicle it was! So we were away—or
thought we were.

We'd had a mental picture of a caravan with a top

which would pull back—similar to the ones we saw nightly on television as political candidates wound their way among the crowds. But on close inspection we discovered that the only way I could come 'out through the top' at it were, was through a fifteen-inch square ventilator in the roof. As we sat in the caravan gazing up at it, almost in despair, the men declared 'You'll never be able to get up through there!' 'Well, let's have a go,' I said, determined not to be beaten at the last minute. By twisting my shoulders through diagonally as someone hoisted me up I just managed it!

Then someone else had the bright idea that we should fasten a pair of high steps to the floor; from there I would be able to speak through the microphone we'd already hired, and rest my legs at the same time.

Next we needed posters to go on the van. And within a very few days a most co-operative (and supportive!) sign writer had produced a huge one which covered both sides, and carried the colourful slogans—CHILDREN AT RISK! VOTE FOR THE CANDIDATE WHO WILL FIGHT FOR DECENCY. Then there was the question of who should drive the van and look after the domestic side. It was at this point that Kay and Steve Stevens, with whom we had worked for many years both in Britain and in Australia, arrived just in time to come with me. And within a week we were away.

Next we had to make sure that the caravan would make maximum impact as we moved slowly through busy streets—and that meant making arrangements with the police in each town we visited. They were very helpful.

One of the many miracles of that trip occurred when we drew up in a lay-by outside Luton, Mr Graham Bright's constituency, to meet with the local newspapers and the police. Just as we stopped, a car drew up behind us. Out of it came David Atkinson, M.P. for Bourne-mouth and, before entering Parliament, chairman of one of the National VALA branches and therefore a very good friend of ours. He had come up behind our caravan with all its vivid covering as it sailed down the motorway and guessed who was inside! It turned out that he had left his own safe constituency to come and support Graham Bright whose seat was very marginal.

He led us to the Conservative Party Offices. There we met Mr Bright, and told him of our hope that whoever was successful in the ballot for Private Members' Bills would use it to introduce a Bill to control 'video nasties'. The media recorded our meeting—particularly the local Press—and one cannot doubt that his public com-mitment to such legislation played a key role in boosting his majority from a few hundred to 5,000! Candidates in the other fifteen constituencies we visited made much the same promise.

Then came the election, the return of a new Conserva-tive government and the ballot for Private Members' Bills. My M.P., Sir Antony Buck Q.C., arranged for me to attend the ballot, and as I walked up the red stair-carpet to the committee room on the first floor of the House of Commons, I prayed—that an M.P., sympa-thetic to a Bill to control such videos, would come at least in the top ten. Only that could give us reasonable grounds for hope—parliamentary time is always at a premium.

I sat there as the parliamentary officials arrived. On the table was a container with the names of over 600 M.P.s inside. I held my breath as a hand went in to draw out the first name. And which was the name he withdrew? None other than that of Mr Graham Bright! I think everyone knows how he was successful in getting his Video Recordings Bill on to the Statue Book in July

1984. (See Appendix 3.)

But there was much more to be done before that was to happen. First, we had to alert people to the need to persuade and encourage their M.P.s to support the Bill. So about 150 letters were sent to local and provincial newspapers around the country. We set out the nature and the size of the problem, emphasizing particularly the threat to the children. We were not talking about a few 'naughty' discs, but an international trade of frightening proportions which posed a considerable threat not only to health of mind and heart but also of body.

The story of Mark[1] is one that I have quoted time and time again, and it never loses its impact either on me or anyone else. It is as true now as when I first read the story that Mark's sufferings alone should be enough to move us, not only to profound pity—and guilt—but to action. And, of course, he is by no means alone.

Mark was a frail-looking boy of thirteen from an unsettled home whose father was 'violent one day, passive the next'. Mark had seen his mother beaten.

His father bought a video recorder and joined a video club, 'regularly bringing home for family consumption the latest XX-rated video films'. The boy watched an increasing number of these films with his father until well into the night—often seeing 'the best bits' repeated in vivid slow motion.

Consequently he found it hard to sleep. When he did he had nightmares. When he got up, he would watch the video again instead of having his breakfast, and he would often rush his supper in order to watch again.

The effect of all this upon his state of mind and body was appalling, though totally predictable. Dark patches under his eyes became a permanent feature. He lost

[1] *Times Educational Supplement* (21 October 1983).

weight. His school work suffered because he was too tired to concentrate.

He couldn't 'take in' new work, and his handwriting became illegible. His voice and his hands would shake and he would 'laugh nervously and become easily excited' as he talked about the latest film he had seen, the violence of which he would describe in an almost incoherent fashion.

In the words of his teacher:

> All aspects of Mark's academic, emotional and even physical development were affected. His writing focused on describing the latest tale of horror; his art work became a disturbing visual rendering of a mind which was obsessed with violence, with drawings full of torn bodies, blood and individuals killing one another. His emotional stability had notably deteriorated: he was aggressive, moody and tearful, and had become withdrawn and pallid.

The teacher, who acknowledged that because of his home situation Mark's behaviour could not be blamed entirely upon watching violent videos, said there could be no doubt that this had made a very considerable contribution to the deterioration which was so marked. Apparently a similar deterioration was noted in one of his friends who had only been exposed to such material for a weekend.

The fact that the school was able to intervene and ensure that Mark no longer had access to such films meant that there was some improvement in his condition; but—as the teacher asks—'How much permanent damage has been done to a child who was already emotionally disturbed?' May we be forgiven.

The BBC transmitted a programme about 'video nasties' ('Open Space' BBC2 June 22nd 1984) in which John Smyth, Q.C. and I participated. Among those in the audience was a father who spoke of an experience within his own family. One Saturday, his twelve-year old son went to spend the morning with a friend. When he came home he was not interested in his lunch, nor later in his tea. By this time his parents had concluded that he was probably sickening for something and got him off early to bed. About midnight they were awakened by him making dreadful noises in his bedroom. They rushed in to see what was the matter.

The boy was kneeling screaming beside his bed with his head down, banging his fists upon the floor. He just went on and on, unable to tell them what was the matter, so they took him into their bed, and held him tight until, in the early hours of the morning, he fell asleep. They had to do this for several weeks before he was able to sleep alone again, and even then he would sometimes shout and cry in his sleep. Bit by bit, the full horror of the 'video nasty' he had seen at his friend's house came out and, in the telling, a certain healing took place.

It was obvious, from the appearance and manner of these parents (both of whom were on the programme and spoke to me afterwards) that they were deeply caring people who would, under no circumstances, have had such videos in their own home or allowed their child to go where he would see one if they had known in advance. Indeed, the same was true of the parents of the other boy.

One could, also, mention the eleven-year old boy who took his mother's tranquillizers after watching 'video nasties' (*Daily Telegraph* 26 April 1984) and the eleven-year old who lived in such fear of a mutilated corpse bursting from his bedroom cupboard that 'he locked his wardrobe, hid the key and refused to go into his bedroom' and according to the *Wolverhampton Express and Star* was still, eight months later, 'too afraid to sleep in the dark'. Incidentally, it was reported that the boy was one of more than 150 children aged between ten and eighteen who regularly watched X-rated films at a local cinema club.

Just how widespread the problems created by 'video horrors' are was demonstrated to a Parliamentary Select Committee on Education, Science and the Arts, when the Committee was told of a school where children aged nine and ten were asleep at their desks at 10.30am. The teacher had told Mr Harry Greenway, M.P. for Ealing South, that he hadn't the heart to wake them because this is the only sleep they can get. He went on to say that on a school visit he had learnt that about eighty per cent of the children's families had videos, and many stayed up until midnight or 1:00am to watch them. Also Committee members were told of one recent episode at a Cardiff junior school when all but one of a class of eight-year olds had admitted watching a 'particularly horrific' late-night movie. Apparently the remaining child listened while his parents were commended. Then he announced that they had videotaped the film so that he could see it when he went home that evening!

Miss Joan Davenport, head teacher of a Manchester primary school and a member of the NUT executive, told the committee that many of her pupils watched video recordings very late at night or had TV sets in their bedrooms. 'By lunchtime many of them are very, very tired and some of them come to school at nine o'clock in the morning yawning.' She stressed that it was important that teachers should be able to meet and talk to parents about the problem and to liaise with other professionals, including health visitors.

These stories—and there are many more—filled us all with a determination to ensure that such blight on the lives of the young would be removed. The Conservatives were back in power—and we knew that we had the strong support of the Prime Minister, Margaret Thatcher, among others. So how could we mobilize wide support in the parliamentary party—there was no shortage of it in the country? 'What about holding "fringe" meetings at the Conservative Party Conference?' we suddenly wondered. But how and what had we in the way of 'ammunition'? Only our voices and our commitment. It was not enough. We needed to be able to *illustrate* what we were talking about—indeed if we could *show* the true nature of the problem we probably wouldn't need to talk at all!

Mercifully we were able to seek the help of someone in a position to put together a short tape, running for about six minutes, which contained extracts from three different 'video nasties'. These particular videos had not been found obscene in the courts, and so we were within the law—although a member of the 'anticensorship' lobby tried to get me arrested! Politicians and Conservative Party activists packed our twice-a-day showings. 'Officially' obscene or not, the video was enough to make them ashen-faced and sick. I sat to one side and slightly behind the screen, in order to ensure that I was able to carry on!

Of course we had never been involved with anything like this before and had no idea how many, if any, conference delegates would attend our meetings—especially as they were being held in a hotel away from the conference building, and involved a walk through the most stormy of weather! I should add that the fact that we were able to hold them at all witnessed, again, to the hand of the Lord in the project. When I first rang to enquire, six weeks before the conference opened, about the possibility of such 'fringe' meetings I was told that it was almost the last day on which I could book them!

The BBC and ITN television news teams who covered our meetings were very deeply shocked at what they saw, and the interest of the media continued throughout. Channel 4 did an interview, BBC2 gave three minutes—a long time in view of all that was happening at a conference which included the Cecil Parkinson débâcle. Among the Press was Carol Thatcher who wrote a special piece for the *Daily Telegraph*, while a journalist from France's *Le Matin* attended our meetings and did a long interview with me, as did assorted local radio stations.

Possibly the most unexpected visitor was the accredited representative of *Pravda*, the Russian newspaper, who clearly took a great interest in what was going on. I saw him hanging around—though I had no idea who he was—while I was having lunch with a member of the conference. When I had to leave rather hastily he sat down in the seat I had vacated and started to speak very intensely to my friend. The gist of his remarks was that he was very anxious that I should know that Russia was very much opposed to all that we were fighting against, and could that message be passed on to me! One knows, of course, that the Communists understand the destructive nature of pornography and that is why they are so strongly opposed to its dissemination in Russia. One also knows that, for the same reason, Communist sympathizers in the West do everything they can to ensure its availability in their own countries.

And we also wrote to the Queen! In reply, her Private Secretary wrote, 'The Queen does indeed share your concern that children should not be exposed to violence and pornography, whether on film or under any other circumstances', and that my letter to her was being 'referred to the Home Secretary for his attention'. That really did lift our hearts. Without any doubt the Home Secretary would have to give anything brought to his attention by the Queen very special attention! But I move too quickly.

Postscript

This is no time to rest on our laurels! *The Video Trade Weekly* (March 4th 1985) carried a report of a meeting held to establish an independent body made up of civil liberties groups, 'celebrity trustees', the Video Trade Association, some M.P.s and members of the House of Lords, to monitor the working of the Video Recordings Act.

The chairman of this group is Lord Houghton of Sowerby, who tried very hard to kill the Video Recordings Bill when it was debated in the House of Lords. We would be wise to keep an eye on its activities!

CHAPTER 3

Children at Risk

The campaign to get legislation to control 'video nasties' on to the Statute Book was launched in August 1980 in our response to the Williams Report on Obscenity and Film Censorship (see Appendix 4). In a letter to the Home Secretary we called on the Government to introduce immediate legislation to control video pornography, and described it as 'a booming industry and the biggest threat to the quality of life in Britain'. We were highly critical of the Williams Report because we felt it was preoccupied with theory and lacking in compassion and understanding of the effect of pornography on people and relationships. We described the Committee's recommendation that hard core pornography (including bestiality) should be available in restricted shops to anyone over the age of seventeen as 'extraordinarily unimaginative and unbelievably naive'. We included letters we had received from parents of children affected by pornography. None more vividly illustrates the reason for our concern than the following:

> With regard to the latest attempts to clean up and tidy all the very loose ends on the subject of what gives offence and what does not; whether people are harmed, or not harmed,

by the still abundant supply of visual sexual material, I will try in some measure to convey to you some of the misery endowed on my little family group by the influences brought to bear by hard core pornography.

My husband and I both served and survived in the last war and our joy since then has been in successfully raising our children to become useful and worthy members of society. Our elder son is an Environmental Health Officer and the younger, a teacher of Biology; but our autumn years now have become marred by worry and constant care and attention of our 16 year old daughter who suffers with Anorexia Nervosa. At the moment she weighs 6¾ stones, at her worst she was 4¾ stones, and but for the skill and care of our doctors and the Grace of God, she would have died. Her normal weight was, and should be, roughly 8¼ stones; she should have 'sat' her 'O' level examinations, but, alas, almost two years have been spent in and out of hospitals. Needless to say she has been robbed of many opportunities. Elizabeth was being independently educated, but with such a loss of time and such a steep rise in school fees, we know we cannot afford to resume the same course of schooling.

What, you will be asking, has all this to do with the law as is now being questioned, on obscenity? It is my belief that pornography has almost robbed us of our beautiful and talented daughter. It transpired that whilst she was under psychotherapy, she revealed that boys at school had got hold of some offensive Danish mail-order type of material (believed taken from one of their parents' bedrooms!) Thus suitably excited and stimulated, they wanted then to see if the female genitalia did really look like the pictures, and so our daughter was the one that had to be pinned and held for exploration. Not quite rape—and yet was it? An experience that made her reject her beautiful female body and life in general. If her weight does not soon become normal and remain stable, she could become sterile.

Elizabeth will need the help of her Consultant Psychia

trist for a long time yet. A thoughtful, pretty and talented girl, we are encouraged by the medical world to lead as normal a family life as we can and are venturing on holiday abroad in three weeks' time—a treat we hardly dare permit ourselves, as the illness apart, we are also self-employed. Elizabeth, we know, will go through mental agony at meal times in the hotel, and we shall have excuses to make for lack of appetite, etc. but we also hope that the holiday could prove a turning point.

Obviously, man's appetite for food and sexual gratification are comforts closely linked, and so therefore, I shall never understand the need to so debase the human body, and the female in particular. If the flow of obscene material of any kind from Scandinavian countries could be stemmed, and too, if some of the 'girlie' or soft porn books removed from the newsagents, I for one would feel a little happier in the knowledge that perhaps other girls entering puberty would not have to go through the same torment. Perhaps other parents too could be spared the heartbreak.

Elizabeth's mother

The near-tragedy of Elizabeth—she was saved only by the great caring and perception of her parents—underlines only too well the cost in personal lives of the kind of licence which characterizes our society. I am constantly reminded of the quotation from Mark's Gospel: 'And whosoever shall offend one of these little ones that believe in me, it is better for him that a millstone were hanged about his neck, and he were cast into the sea' (Mk 9:42).

Support for Mr Graham Bright's Bill to control 'video nasties' flooded in not only from ordinary people but also from public figures representing church, State and the law. I have mentioned Mrs Thatcher's support. It came also from the Archbishop of Canterbury, Dr Runcie, when he opened the House of Lords' debate on 'video nasties'. He declared that it was right to be deeply concerned about the incidence of violent crime in our society, with the problems of prison overcrowding and with the seeming failure to find solutions: 'For too long the public has seemed to want to push these matters under the carpet.' He went on, 'Perhaps the very size of the problems has now woken us up to the fact that there is work which not only can be done but which must be done, and for which resources must be found.' Dr Runcie added: 'It is work which should start in the home, be continued in the schools, and which should involve every community. For the heart of this matter is the question of the kind of moral values on which we wish the life of our nation to be based. Only limited good can be done by Acts of Parliament, important as they are. Responsibility for these problems must be accepted by each one of us as individuals and by the community as a whole.'

He identified three main areas of concern—'video nasties', which, it was clear from a recent showing to M.P.s in the House of Commons, was 'a deeply disturbing phenomenon'; the influence of television; and the problem of violence induced by alcohol.

Supporting the Video Recordings Bill which had already been given a second reading in the Commons, Dr Runcie said 'A society which genuinely wants to curb the incidence of violent crime must confront this frightening influence for evil.'

In the same debate Lord Hailsham, the Lord Chancellor, agreed with Dr Runcie that parents and the community had a responsibility. But he stressed: 'If we see what we see on page three of a newspaper or in other media let us not be altogether surprised if on page one or five we read a melancholy recital of homosexual murders, rapes, crimes like the Ripper's woundings, burglaries, kidnappings or child abuse either by violence or sex.'

Also participating in the debate was Lord Lane, the Lord Chief Justice, who suggested that 'we might reintroduce conscience and reintroduce the devil'. He went on to say that unemployment was regarded as one of the facts influencing the crime rate, but that there were many other reasons: easier divorce (soon to become easier still), broken homes, easier abortion, and the pill at the age of eleven and twelve, the abuse and import of hard drugs, the part alcohol played in many crimes, and the increase in horror and filth through degrading film and television programmes. 'It is regrettable that some of the television authorities present violence and obscenity as a form of entertainment,' Lord Lane said. If that happened, very soon violence and obscenity became accepted by the weaker brethren as the norm, and it was they whom the House of Lords were debating.

'It seems horrifying,' the Lord Chief Justice continued, 'that it was only when Scotland Yard put together some horror videos to show M.P.s in the Commons that voices started to be raised. Did it really require live cannibalism to make people realize what the horror videos were? It is sad to see the paralysed acquiescence of ordinary society.'

Such a stand by men of that calibre strongly undergirded the campaign both in the country and in the House of Commons. But there were serious problems nevertheless.

The main argument during the Committee stage of the Bill centred around the question of whether or not films given an 'R' (Restricted) 18 certificate should be banned by the Bill. The amendment which would have achieved this was introduced by Sir Bernard Braine, Conservative M.P. for Castle Point. Sir Bernard was an immense help throughout the whole of the parliamentary campaign. And not only Sir Bernard; Mr David Mellor, Under Secretary at the Home Office, gave us an enormous amount of official and unofficial help throughout the campaign, and, by no manner of means least, during the Committee stage of the Bill.

The fact that Mrs Thatcher had made known her anxiety that the Bill should not only get on the Statute Book but also turn out to be a really effective measure reinforced Mr Mellor's own deep concern and sympathy for the Bill. He too put his finger on the heart of the matter when he told the Committee that if 18 R videos were sold to adults in shops, they were bound to be shown in the home, where children might see them.

Speaking to the Committee Sir Bernard said:

There is a curious opinion abroad that somehow one can draw a line between the worst form of video nasty and what is called soft porn, or to use a new term in the trade, 'video naughties'.

Every member of this committee must have been shocked by the Old Bailey trial last week, in which a husband and wife pleaded guilty to committing sexual offences on their own children, a boy of 10 and a girl of 11, after allowing them to watch pornographic videos.

The parents are in prison, the children are in care, and the judge described pornographic videos as a vicious intrusion into the home.

In the end we have to think of the protection of children. Once outside the shop, control of these videos will be lost. I believe that children will be damaged by this material, however straight the sex may be.

But, unfortunately, in the event Government-backed moves to ban the sale of pornographic video cassettes which did not necessarily fit the description of 'video

nasties', were defeated in Committee by eleven votes to
five. We may yet see—perhaps before very long—how
disastrous the failure of the Committee to heed these
warnings was.

The defeat of Sir Bernard's initiative was a great
disappointment to us. We were now left with a totally
illogical situation. A child cannot see 18 R material
passed by the British Board of Film Censors in a sex
cinema, but will be perfectly free to do so in his own
home. That this does happen in a disturbingly high
number of homes we have already seen. So the battle is
by no means over, and the warning that 'the price of
freedom is eternal vigilance' has never been more true
than today. It would indeed be a tragedy if people were
to feel that because we have a Video Recordings Act on
the Statute book, 'That's that.' It by no means is. Not
least, because at the time of writing it looks as though
there would well be considerable delay before the Video
Recordings Act comes into effect.

The Act is concerned solely with the classification of
videos. Any video which fails to obtain a classification is
automatically illegal. The number of videos to be viewed
and classified makes it an enormous task and one which
makes very great demands upon those whose job it is to
watch film after film. We—and they—have to be very
conscious of the desensitization which inevitably takes
place when people are continuously closeted in a small
dark room watching one dubious film after another.
Everything becomes relative. A particular video may
not be quite as extreme therefore it is given a certificate
—whereas if it had been seen before the previous one
then it may well have been refused a certificate. The
bounds of acceptability are constantly pushed back, not
necessarily by deliberate intent but because of the
inevitable corruption of judgement which results.

I don't think anyone, whether members of the public, of Parliament or of the video trade itself had any conception of how complicated the whole process of classification was to prove!

In the first place, as I write in the autumn of 1984, the British Board of Film Censors have to tackle the task of *viewing* before being able to classify around seven to eight thousand videos, and expect to have added to that number something like another two thousand tapes a year! The great majority of these will be thoroughly decent and enjoyable films but will still need to be classified so that everyone buying a video will know precisely into which category it fits—whether it is universally acceptable (U) or at the other extreme (18 R—a classification which, as I have already said, gives considerable cause for concern).

As an indication of just how complex and demanding the job is, we only have to consider the trade in ethnic videos; for example, videos are produced—in the appropriate languages—for the market that exists among the 100,000 Chinese in this country, and for that among the Muslims, the Hindus, the Greeks, the Turks and so on.

The fact that a film has to be given *two* certificates, one for the cinema and one to guarantee that it is 'suitable for showing in the home' as the Video Recording Act requires, underlines again the size of the task which has been laid upon the British Board of Film Censors. It seems beyond doubt that, far from coming into effect in November 1984 as was originally envisaged, it may well be two or even three years before that happens.

Certainly at the time of writing there is considerable anxiety about the situation, and there are even fears that the Act itself may go by default. One very much hopes that this may not be so. But how deeply one also feels regret—more, shame. As a society we have been prepared, albeit sometimes unwillingly, to come to terms with so much that is dehumanizing and destructive, let alone anti-Christian in its impact. Now we are faced with a situation which is almost impossible to resolve.

And do we ever think, with at least some compassion, of those who on our behalf sit closeted hour after hour, day after day, week, month and year after week, month and year with grossly violent, obscene and perverted images?

Just how great is the need for really effective action to control videos was highlighted again in the last days of February 1985 when the appalling case of the so-called 'Fox' was heard in Leeds Crown Court. This made huge headlines in all the newspapers, which gave tremendous prominence not only to what they called the 'Fox's' 'reign of terror' but also to the words of Mr Justice Canefield. In sentencing Malcolm Fairley the judge said to him 'You have desecrated and defiled men and women, old and youthful, in their own homes which you have then pillaged. I am satisfied that you are a decadent advertisement for the evils of pornographers. But they will want to forget you.' Fairley was sentenced to six life sentences for the rapes and burglaries he had committed, and to a further eighty-two years for crimes which the judge described as depraved and wicked.

It is not for me to comment further on a case which tells its own dreadful story, but I think one thing has to be said and I said it at the time. It is this. 'Terrible as the "Fox's" crimes have been, it ill becomes any of us to take a holier-than-thou attitude. It could well be that if successive governments had responded to the calls that have been consistently made over these last years for more effective obscenity legislation those crimes may not have been committed. The burden of guilt lies on us all.'

The case highlighted the quite unsatisfactory situation as far as the Video Recordings Act was concerned. Eight months after the passing of the Act, none of the videos which stimulated anxiety in the first place had been classified. The order designating the British Board of Film Censors as the classifying body had still not been laid before Parliament (it wasn't until June 1985) and therefore that body had not begun its task as far as those videos were concerned.

The very videos which inspired the 'Fox' to act out his sadistic sex fantasies were available at shops throughout the country. One of them showed the violent rape of a woman by a man wearing a balaclava helmet —as the 'Fox' did—and carrying a shotgun—as the 'Fox' did. And yet there are still people who deny the truth that people *are* affected, for better or worse, by what they see and what they feed their minds on.

The horror of this case called to mind the tragedy of the Moors murder case in which little children were the victims of Myra Hindley and Ian Brady, who themselves used pornography as a stimulation for their perverted activities. The 'Cambridge rapist' a few years ago was also addicted to pornography.

The trouble is that we forget. The horror of such cases brings our own protective mechanism into effect. It is all too horrible to think about. Yet if it *is* true that we all carry the guilt because of our failure to build adequate legislation to deal with the problem, and also because we don't really want to know, then we surely have to face that weakness in ourselves and in our society. Members of Parliament *will* act if we demand that they should, and if we give them no rest till they have.

It is more than understandable that people recoil from being involved in such a corrupt trade. I know St Paul's words, 'Whatsoever things are pure, whatsoever things are lovely...think on these things.' And indeed we should, for therein lies peace. But we also have to think of Jesus' words. He told us that 'whoso shall offend one of these little ones...it were better for him that a millstone were hanged about his neck, and he were cast into the sea.'

To keep one's mind unsullied, while at the same time doing battle with the corruption in our society, is a profound challenge.

CHAPTER 4

Censorship—A Wicked Word

Time and time again, whether it's been a matter of
speaking in public, writing letters or appearing on television, or just chatting personally with people, friends
and enemies alike, I have had to realize that there is no
alternative to hard fact and well thought-out logic
(something which does not come naturally to me!)
particularly, for example, when discussing the wide
ramifications of the question of censorship.

It's always very interesting to notice how that word
can raise more hackles than blasphemous and obscene
ones—particularly among secular and educational
audiences. This is due in part to its historical ramifications, witness the horrors of the Inquisition and
Nazi Germany, and of course to the censorship which
exists in so many countries today.

If we are to deal effectively with this issue, it is I think
important to realize that the real and understandable
fear that people have of the dangers implicit in certain
aspects of censorship has been played upon quite un-
scrupulously by those who were, and are, opposed to
our work. They have claimed that we desire either
collectively or individually, to *be* the censors and to have
the power to 'ban' this, that, or the other. How do we

answer that accusation?

First of all, by making it clear that we are totally opposed to *political* censorship. And it is well to remember that this can manifest itself not only in the dramatic burning of books but in far more subtle ways. For instance, by so setting up a TV or radio discussion programme that certain views are 'censored out' by exclusion and other views advocated by the tone of an interviewee's voice and the length of time given to the protagonists. An apparently minor example, but one worth noting, is whether or not the same interviewee has the first *and* the last word!

Secondly, we need to emphasize that in no way would we seek the power to prejudge or ban a programme— what we are concerned about is that public pressure should be put upon producers and others involved so that they fulfil the obligations laid upon them 'not to offend against good taste and decency'. These obligations are laid upon the broadcasting authorities by *Parliament*—not by us or any one else! It is the broadcasters who are called to exercise censorship—to say 'No' to this sequence and 'Cut' to that one before they ever get on to the screen. And this is where public pressure should have its effect.

Thirdly, in making our voice heard, either collectively or individually, we are actually performing a service to the broadcasters. How are they to know whether or not they 'give offence to public feeling' (as they are obliged not to), unless there is continuing expression of distaste when in fact offence has been given? And one should say again how important it is that we all take the trouble to praise what is good as well as criticize what is bad. After all it is only through continuing inter-communication of this kind that professional broadcasters can come to understand just how their own values and standards compare with those of certain of their 'consumers'.

It is surely important also to expose the invalidity of the 'no censorship at any cost' philosophy. For can anyone in their right mind agree with the proposition that there should be no limits imposed on the public presentation of sex and violence and in the use of language? This, in the last resort, could mean accepting even the public display of the violation of children and the use of television to advocate violent elimination of coloured people, perhaps along the lines of the Nazi atrocities against the Jews. It could mean freedom, too, to batter the sensitivities of young and old alike with an undiluted stream of the foulest obscenities. And just about everyone would revolt against that.

We have already seen how the radical left are convinced that sexual permissiveness and moral relaxation are primary conditions for the establishment of the 'alternative society'; and if any of us think that the increasing acceptance of blasphemies and obscenities is simply part of an evolving contemporary society, we are being dangerously naive.

Many will remember the terrible tragedy of the shooting and killing of students by the National Guard at Kent State University in the USA. James Mitchener, that highly accomplished historical writer, published a book shortly afterwards called *Kent State—What Happened and Why*. In it he set out the many pressures which students experienced in the so-called 'liberal' sixties, and he made a comment about the deliberate strategy which lay behind the propagation of obscenity and blasphemy. He wrote:

Numerous committed revolutionaries have preached that the debasement of language is one of the most powerful agencies for the destruction of existing society. They argue, 'if you destroy the word, you can destroy the system,' and they have consciously set out to do both.

This was another example of how those who are in a position to understand these things in a way and with a depth not given to the average person can help us to understand the deeper implications of what is happening in the world in which we live. We do need to grasp fully the fact that we are engaged in an ideological battle as well as a moral one. I would even go so far as to say that if we do not understand the nature of the first we shall be shorn of many of the weapons with which to fight the second.

The question now arises: do we have the right to expect government and law, while protecting the free flow of ideas, to establish sufficient control to ensure that society remains coherent and capable of resisting the pressures of that statistically minute group who are committed to its destruction? I believe, profoundly, that we *do*. Censorship, effectively but sparingly used, is a liberal concept since it could serve to protect the life style of the vast majority.

The civil libertarians object to censorship on the grounds that no one has the right to interfere in the 'private' affairs of others. 'Let a man go to hell in his own way,' they say. But, whom do they take with them, and what rights do the victims have?

Perhaps the most notorious crime associated with violent pornography—apart from the 'Moors Murders' —was the attempted assassination of US Governor George Wallace in 1972. At the trial a quotation from the gunman's diary was read out. In it he had written 'I saw *Clockwork Orange* and thought of getting Wallace during the film.' After he had been found guilty he was asked if he had anything to say. His reply? 'All I wish is that you had protected me from myself.' I'm sure that Governor Wallace, who still lives in a wheelchair, thinks so too.

It is almost unbelievable now that parliamentarians in 1959 genuinely believed that Mr Roy Jenkin's private member's Bill, which became the Obscene Publications Act, really would tighten up legislation to control obscenity, given the fact that it has proved so unworkable. It's also worth noting that the bill was envisaged solely as a means of controlling the *printed* word, since the type of pictorial pornography which has increasingly littered our bookshelves in the years since was then virtually unknown. In fact the object of the 1959 Act was 'to amend the law relating to the publication of obscene matter; to provide for the protection of literature; *and to strengthen the law concerning pornography*' (my italics). I'm tempted to say that if it were not so tragic it would be funny!

The exact words of the clause in the Act which has proved so ineffective are as follows. An article is declared to be obscene 'if its effect, or the effect of any one of its parts which, if taken as a whole, is such as to deprave or corrupt persons who are likely, having regard to all the relevant circumstances, to read, see or hear the matter contained or embodied in it'.

This phraseology, far from tightening up the law as was originally intended, has throughout the last twenty-five years proved hopelessly ineffective. The responsibility laid upon a jury was one which became increasingly difficult to fulfil. How can one *prove* that something is likely to deprave or corrupt? Members of the jury were asked countless times by defending counsel whether *they* were depraved or corrupted by what they had seen. It was an entirely natural response to think, 'Well, no, *I'm* not depraved'—and to draw the logical conclusion: if they were not, what right had they to assume that anyone else would be?

The words 'Those who are likely...to read, see or hear the said publication' lands the prosecution in further trouble. Time and again the defence was put forward that the 'dirty raincoat brigade' which bought such material was corrupted already, and therefore was unlikely to be further depraved. No word about what happened to the material after it had been discarded by its purchaser! Left behind in toilets? What if the next 'gent' to enter should be a ten or twelve-year old boy? Dumped behind bushes in a park for innocent children to pick up? Left in a drawer in a parent's bedroom for suspicious teenagers to forage for? Endless evidence that this actually happens leaves one in no doubt that the biggest and most important task that we all have to tackle, as far as legislation is concerned, is to work for the effective tightening up of the obscenity law. But I will come back to that in a later chapter.

I want first to deal with some of the propaganda which was, and still is used by the libertarians to condition public opinion to an acceptance of a situation with which no Christian society should ever have come to terms. But even as I say that I am deeply conscious of the very great difficulties that face the average man and woman, busily concerned as they are with the demands of everyday life.

We in National VALA have been very blessed in that we have enjoyed the co-operation of highly experienced and trained Christian academics such as, for example, Dr John Court, an Englishman working at Flinders University, Australia. He spent several years of his life researching the *truth* which lay behind so many of the myths which were deliberately propagated in the sixties and seventies by those with vested financial and political interests in conditioning people to believe that pornography was 'liberating'. Their propaganda, not least because it was given such publicity in the media, put down deep roots into our subconscious—let alone conscious—thinking about these matters.

Take the question of Denmark. We hear far less about the myth of the Danish sexual utopia today, but those who were responsible for its creation have seen it sink deep into our common psyche, and anyone who wants to be in a position to write and speak knowledgeably about the cultural—let alone the moral—history of the last few decades does need to have certain facts at their fingertips. Otherwise the slogan 'It's all a matter of personal taste', which trips so easily off the tongue, will be very difficult to rebut.

Dr Court went to Denmark several times during the seventies in his academic capacity, and it was he who exposed and tabulated the various Danish myths which were not only so powerfully conditioning public, media, even parliamentary opinion, but were being widely and successfully quoted by defence lawyers in successive obscenity trials here in Britain and elsewhere. These cases continuously undermined what effectiveness the Obscenity Law possessed, thus providing the basis of the situation we face today.

One of the most frequently quoted myths was that 'people get bored with pornography when it is readily available'. This view was held by the Danish Minister of Justice, who was responsible for the repeal of many of his country's censorship laws. 'Allow obscene literature and people will soon tire of it, the illicit attraction having been removed' he persuaded the Danish Parliament and people. But 'liberalization' of the law had precisely the opposite effect. Interest shifted from 'normal' erotica into homosexual and bondage material, and into sado-masochism and bestiality. The same thing has happened in every country where pornography has been 'liberated'!

Another very persuasive argument was that 'only the tourists buy porn'. Dr Court discovered the basis of such a claim was no more than a 'pilot' experiment carried out by one Dr Berl Kutchinsky, a Danish researcher who gained international fame (many would say notoriety) for his role in freeing pornography from many of its legal restraints not only in his native country, but also throughout the free world.

Kutchinsky himself admitted when I talked to him that the people he used in this piece of research were 'more experienced with pornography than the average population of Copenhagen', and he went on to admit that his findings were 'unsuitable' as grounds for serious debate! What is more this particular myth, as Kutchinsky himself acknowledged, was based upon his very superficial sampling of only thirty of the sixty sex shops operating in Copenhagen at that time. He stood in each for half an hour, watching the customers as they came in, but not speaking to them. This was the basis of his claim that 'foreigners accounted for most of the purchases'! Such is the flimsiness—if not the frivolity—of the 'evidence' upon which a social/cultural revolution has been based. And all the time, it has to be remembered, there was a quite deliberate policy of censorship, ridicule, and misrepresentation directed at attempts by people such as ourselves to establish the truth of the matter.

Another very persuasive myth which was repeated over and over again was that it was 'perfectly possible to protect children, so therefore adults should be free to hear, read and see what they like'. All experience, personal and professional, shows this to be quite false. This we have dealt with at length elsewhere; but perhaps this is the place to recall the United Nations *Declaration of the Rights of the Child*. This states that:

> The child shall enjoy special protection and shall be given opportunities and facilities by law and by other means, to enable him to develop physically, mentally, spiritually and socially in a healthy and normal manner and in conditions of freedom and dignity. In the enactment of laws for this purpose the best interests of the child shall be paramount.

We forget or deliberately ignore this at our own peril— and that of our children.

Perhaps the most pernicious myth was the one that declared: 'When pornography is made readily available, then sex crimes diminish drastically.'

Certainly, statistically speaking, there has been a marked decrease in the number of less violent sex crimes in Denmark. But what lies behind these figures? The simple fact is that eleven categories of sex crime were removed from the Danish statute book in 1969. And without *law* there cannot be *crime!* I'm always conscious of the expressions of dawning comprehension that pass across the faces in the audience when I make what is, after all, a perfectly obvious statement but one which has been assiduously censored out of Press and television discussion on 'The State of Denmark'. And when one looks at the figures published by the Copenhagen police for rape and attempted rape—crimes still on the statute book—a very different picture emerges.

Dr Inge Krogh, chief psychiatrist at the Nyborg Mental Hospital in Denmark, sent us in September 1980 her comments on the Report of the Home Office Committee on Obscenity and Film Censorship chaired by Professor Bernard Williams (November 1979). She was particularly interested in what the Committee had said about the situation in Denmark, not least in its claim that, following relaxation in the law, there had been a heavy decline of interest in pornography. Dr Krogh told us that this was:

>...Not true. There are still a large number of shops with pornography only. A district in Copenhagen, Vesterbro, has been completely changed into a district with porno-shops, massage clinics and prostitution. The streets are characterized by drug addicts, alcoholic abuse, and violence. Formerly it was a residential quarter: now only a few guest workers live there. In a street in this district, Istedgade, there are 30 porno-shops with so called 'cinemas', showing non-stop films, in a distance of 400 metres.... In the Copenhagen main street, the *Strøget*, and in most provincial towns there are similar shops and 'cinemas'; e.g. Aalborg with appro. 95,000 inhabitants has five shops and 'cinemas'.

>I have enquired of our Minister of Justice if we could get a provision saying that the window displays in such shops should be covered by black curtains, which I have seen in New York, but he refused.

>There is a provision saying that pornography must not be sold to young people under 16 years of age. I guess that this is unknown for most of the owners of the shops. There is not even a notice about it. I have enquired of the Minister, if he could do something about it, but he refused.

>To get a license to run such a porno-cinema the only demand is that you are a Danish subject. I have enquired the Minister if it is possible to lay down greater demands to the holder of the license, if it is possible to lay down demands on the establishment of these rooms because of the fire risk, and if it is possible to reduce the number of these cinemas, so that the accumulation would not be so big. The Minister refused all these questions.

>In the Copenhagen municipality 60–70 people have the

license to run such sex cinemas. Apart from these shops, where solely pornography is sold, you can see pornographic booklets and cassettes with films and exposures in practically every news-stand all over the country.

In almost every police regulation it is prohibited to display such pictures in public streets but they are. The exposures are usually sex act or nude pictures heavily emphasizing the sexual characters. In a certain news-stand in a provincial town with about 13,000 citizens I objected to the owner about some exposures lying in the window. Then he put matchboxes on the most embarrassing spots and he continues to do so. Perhaps the sale is stimulated by the thought of what is hidden below the matchboxes.

The displays of pornography in proper porno shops as well as news-stands have led to a much changed view on these things. It has been reflected in a change of the weekly magazines, especially those read by children and young people. These magazines, which are read in great numbers by young people under education—also in grammar schools—contains more violence and sex than before, and they must be characterized as semi pornographic.

At the end of her letter to us she quoted some very telling statistics which powerfully underlined the links between pornography and sex crimes. She told how:

A police inspector in one of our larger provincial towns has informed that in 90 per cent of all cases they find pornography by the sex criminals. Recently they have started to take interest in wife battering and rape, and it seems as if much of the violence takes place after pornography has been read.

She then went on to give official statistics regarding the situation in Copenhagen.

In 1970, 47 cases of rape and the like were reported in the police districts of greater Copenhagen; during the years 1971 to 1978 inclusive, the number of reported cases was 101, 83, 87, 94, 97, 101, 110 and 257 respectively. Heterosexual infringement of minors was reported in 1970 as 75 cases. For the years 1971 to 1978 inclusive the number of cases was 87, 79, 77, 142, 123, 82, 124 and 112 respectively.[1]

I have dealt with the Danish situation at some length because I think it is tremendously important that we realize how very organized and completely unscrupulous are those who have much to gain, materially, from the removal of controls both in this country and across the world.

It is true, of course, that the sex shops in Copenhagen have proved a tourist attraction, though not to every tourist! But pornography is equally to be found on bookstalls in the suburbs, while sex shops and live shows are developing in the working-class dormitory suburbs and proliferating in towns far beyond Copenhagen. The clientele for these is undoubtedly local; much printed material is in a Scandinavian language. Add to all this the fact that the mail order business in pornography is recognized to be considerable, and Kutchinsky's conclusions begin to look very insubstantial indeed—especially as pornography and its 'sidekicks' have become part of the economic structure of Denmark.

---

[1] The following up-to-date statistics (countrywide) were sent to us (30th November 1984) by the Parliamentary Group of the Danish Christian People's Party.
The figures for 1977 to 1983 inclusive for rape were, 280, 484, 329, 363, 402, 364 and 505 respectively. Heterosexual infringement of minors for the years 1977 to 1983 inclusive were 265, 229, 252, 228, 257, 210 and 337 respectively.

The thought of child prostitution inevitably arouses a very great repugnance in every normal—let alone Christian—person. Mercifully it is something which, we feel, is unlikely to touch any child of ours.

However, I would suggest, such an assurance should make us more, not less, prepared to face the problem where it exists, and where possible to do something about it. Gitta Sereny, whose first book *The Case of Mary Bell* was most highly praised by the critics, has published a highly disturbing and challenging book[1] about child prostitution in America, Germany and Britain. While I appreciate that not many of us will be in a position to go out and buy it we can all request it at our local libraries.

She demonstrates how about ten per cent of runaway children are so badly alienated from their families that they simply *cannot* go home. Her investigations reveal that it is often a matter of hours before someone has tricked them into selling their only asset.

Gitta Sereny spent very many hours talking to some of these children and their parents and her book carries detailed accounts of what lay behind the child's decision to leave home: and she talked to their parents and did what she could to help them to make a fresh start together.

Some of the stories do have a happy ending, but in others the heartbreak remains and in the end the responsibility devolves upon us all. And it is chastening to realize that by no means all these children are of low intelligence or have been driven out of their homes by brutality. In fact her researches show that the root cause has been the neurotic limitations of thoroughly respectable and even well-meaning parents.

[1] *The Invisible Children* (Andre Deutsch, 1984).

What she has to say about the underlying causes of child prostitution echoes in many ways the theme of this book.

> Most of the causes of child prostitution are to be found in individual character traits and individual deficiencies, some of which may exist independently of societal pressures. But nobody lives in a void, and the young—especially those of them who are particularly vulnerable —are the people most subject to influences from without.
>
> No other age has encouraged violent crime, as ours does, by constantly exploiting it as entertainment. No other age has subjected so many people to such a bombardment of artificial stimulation, so that our children are urged or forced as never before into adult behaviour and pleasures, and are brainwashed into readymade decisions on almost every puzzling subject under the sun, particularly that of sex. Everyday of their lives, from newspapers, magazines, advertisements, pop music, and above all from television, they are presented with images and interpretations of sex which have little to do with its reality. They are supposed to be able to absorb and come to terms with all this without being damaged. Is it possible? Demonstrably, for quite a large number of them, it is not; and that should give us pause.
>
> Although we are accustomed to think that the rejection of traditional values—those of family, religion and disciplined education—by the young is a nearly inevitable part of adolescent rebellion, the children we have met here appear to demonstrate a desperate need for family life, for structure in their environment, and for the kind of support found in a faith or in some degree of intellectual discipline.

Many of us have thought of Sweden as being a very 'free for all' society as far as the availability of pornography, violence and obscenity are concerned. Indeed that *has* been a fair description, but not any more. Sweden is now giving a lead which could well be followed by many other countries—including our own.

Mr Bo Carlsson, then chairman of the Swedish Children's Ombudsmen, was the speaker at National VALA's 1983 Convention when he spoke of the way in which violence in the media affects children and explained how important it was to understand how children are influenced and moulded by their environment, during their upbringing. This is certainly a complex issue, but to simplify it one can say that all settings that surround a child have an influence. The closer the setting is to the child, the more influence it has. Early, the family, or perhaps the mother, plays the most important role. The child's ability and opportunity to come in contact with other settings such as school and friends is very limited. A new development, however, has been the television within the four walls of the home. Small children watch TV from an early age. Television then has become one important factor or setting from which the child early gets to know what is desirable and what is the 'normal' way of life.

Because of the extensive amount of time that the child spends looking at TV and video, the influence of the media plays an important role in the child's socialization process. When we also discover that most of what they view promotes and glorifies violence and other forms of anti-social behaviour we must react.

He went on:

> Today we teach children at school to read a text critically and also, in the best case, to decode the message as we encounter it in newspapers, etc. We do not have such a general education as regards the visual media. In actual fact, we are all practically illiterate when it comes to critical media knowledge. We must, therefore, learn to read and write all over again. That is to say, everyone must be able to see what is behind the visual images and

examine them with a critical eye. A new gigantic literacy campaign must be mounted.

We use legislation today to prevent children from seeing violence or obscene films in the cinema. But we do not think it necessary to prevent them from seeing the same films on TV or video. This is to say the least inconsistent.... Violence is a fact of life and a predominant factor in our societies. This does, however, not mean that we have to conform to it or even give in. There are hopes for a more human world. But to get there we have to fight violence in all its forms and show people that there are other ways of solving conflicts. In this respect, visual media can be a good and useful tool. It is therefore with sadness and anger one sees these media instead do the opposite. Let us together say no to that development, and instead say yes to positive visual media that promote positive values and respect human rights.

In June 1981, a Swedish law was passed which prohibits the commercial renting or showing, to children below fifteen years of age, of films and videograms with detailed and realistic portrayals of violence or threats of violence to human beings or animals. In 1984 Parliament passed another law prohibiting the distribution to adults of films and videograms containing indiscreet and prolonged portrayals of brutal or sadistic violence. And in the meantime—what's been happening elsewhere?

Let us, for example, consider America. The quotation that follows is taken from the *Arizona Republic* (June 8th 1984). Despite the fact that we are told that publication of this report reflects a 'change of attitude' in editorial policy, I find it quite frightening.

Porn peddlers are doing an $8 billion business, and sales are climbing.

More sadistic and violent material is being produced with continued emphasis on 'Kiddie Porn' in which youngsters in their early teens—or even younger—are filmed in sexual acts.

California police recently confiscated 200 such films and a list of thousands of buyers in a raid on just one distributor.

Some 20,000 adult bookstores and nearly 1,000 X-rated movie theatres still operate, but the greatest jump in X-rated material has been among videotapes for the home.

Penalties for producing and distributing porn have increased, including a $100,000 fine and 10 years in prison for a first offense involving children.

Customs seizures of porn material rose 200 per cent last year. However, since smut is so profitable, producers churn out even greater volumes of material.

They're also creating new markets. An audit of the Defense Department's long-distance telephone charges revealed at least $250,000 was for calls to dial-a-porn services.

Many Americans are tempted to say that increased penalties and crackdowns will never stamp out smut. That is another way of saying government cannot legislate morality.

Pornography is a cancer of the spirit which preys on human weakness instead of uplifting the good.

Although there will always be evil in the world, man's duty is to combat it and, when possible, defeat it.

It would be quite wrong of me to conclude what could be a quite depressing chapter without indicating some of the successes—particularly here in Britain—which have been achieved by ordinary people in the fight against, for example, sex shops in their own area.

The Local Government (Miscellaneous Provisions) Act was passed in 1982 (see Appendix 5). Prior to the passing of that Act members of the public, especially parents, who were affronted by the presence of sex shops (often in shopping centres where no one could avoid them) found themselves fighting a losing battle against the powerful international sex trade.

However the new Act, passed on a tide of public concern, put a powerful, though somewhat tedious, weapon into the hands of the police and the public (see Appendix). And it is immensely encouraging to see how people have undertaken with great heart and determination to remove, as far as is humanly and legally possible, this scourge from our midst.

Some of the letters which have come to us underline this very vividly. Here's one from Scotland—

> We in Paisley were shocked to find we had a 'Private Shop' practically on our High Street. We formed a 'Campaign for Common Decency'—we picketed, we collected signatures, we found out who the shareholders were, and we exposed them. We hired a solicitor and he fought and won our case. It took two years and four months to get it closed, but it was worth it.

And from Weston-Super-Mare:

> This is just to share the good news with you, that the Sex Shop in Weston-Super-Mare has been closed within the last few days! There have been many people in Weston praying for this to happen and we see it as an answer to prayer, but would also like to thank you for your part in it. Your advice in the VALA paper (repeated in *Buzz* magazine) was an essential part of the campaign, in warning us of the Licensing Laws which came into effect at such very short notice, almost two years ago.

It goes without saying that this is no time to sit back and rest on our laurels. The burgeoning sex industry has at its disposal vast monetary and legal resources to challenge every aspect of the law. It must be remembered that applications for the renewal of a licence to keep a sex shop—and some local authorities *are* allowing them, if only in reduced numbers—has to be made every year. It follows that the *objection* to the sex shops has to be made every year too! An appalling prospect? Indeed. But even more appalling if we tire of the challenge. Someone has to tire first, and one can only hope that it is the sex barons (see Appendix 9).

The kind of commitment which Christians—and others—have shown is illustrated by Derby's Christian Trade Unionist Association which on April 14th 1983 handed a 3,000 signature petition to the Town Council. One could go on, naming town after town—Glasgow, Coventry, Ryde (4,000 signatures), Croydon, and Portsmouth (where all four sex shops were ordered to shut down). In Preston in early 1984 there was great celebration of a victory over one of Britain's biggest sex shop chains. The London-based Quietlynn Group, which ran 128 shops in England and Wales at the time, lost an appeal against local authorities who refused to license outlets in three major towns.

In Birmingham—where the sex shop situation has always presented a tough challenge—four out of the five sex shops and cinemas faced closure in September 1984, after a crackdown by city councillors. Not unexpectedly they are expected to appeal. It is I think worth quoting from the *Birmingham Evening Mail* (6th September 1984), which gives some flavour of the intensity of the fight put up by both sides.

> The only one of five applications granted a licence by the Birmingham City Council's licensing sub-committee was described as relatively innocuous. There were originally 13 applications from sex shops and cinemas last year when the City Council decided to use new Government laws which give town halls tough control. Eight were

approved initially, although only four are believed to be still in existence. At least two found licence fees of £1,000 too costly. The remaining five were deferred pending a legal test case, taken out by a chain group against six councils. The City Council said it was likely to refuse them, and has now done so in four cases.

Postscript

From the *Weston Mercury*, Friday, November 16th 1984:

From Sex to the Scriptures

The premises of the former sex shop in Weston will in future sell religious books.

The premises, in Meadow Street, have been bought by Ann and Eric Pursey, and are being opened by Mr H. W. King, former director of publicity and public relations for Woodspring District Council, tomorrow at 10 am.

There New Horizons will be selling religious and children's books.

A member of National VALA reported:

At the opening of this shop this morning I heard the following,—'Good clean books—what a change.' 'Wholesome!' 'We have prayed faithfully for two years for a Christian bookshop *on this site*.' 'Why stop our prayers at closing shops?'

Finally, here is an extract from the Community Standards Association Newsletter (Spring 1985).

No Sex Shops in Cornwall

We are happy to be able to tell you that all six local authorities in Cornwall have adopted the powers offered to them under the Local Government (Miscellaneous

Provisions) Act 1983, to ensure that any sex shop or sex cinema wishing to open in Cornwall applies to the local authority for a licence. To the best of our knowledge no such applications have so far been made. We believe that CSA has played its part over the years in helping Cornwall's local authorities and the general public to become more aware of the dangers of pornography in films and magazines and to be more disposed to take a stand against its further distribution.

Sex shops must close

Three sex shops existed in Exeter at the time the Local Government (Miscellaneous Provisions) Bill became law in 1983. Mr Forrow, a full-time nurse and Hon. Secretary of the newly-formed Exeter and District CSA, attributes the success of his campaign to persuade Exeter City Council not to license these, to the number of people praying, to the information he and others provided to the residents of Exeter, and to their response in approaching the City Council themselves. Two shops for which applications for licences had been refused were still trading at the end of 1984. However, the owners of these premises had both made application in the High Court for judicial review of the Council's decision to refuse licences and one of these has been heard and dismissed. The Council is now considering its next course of action. As regards the third shop, the High Court application is likely to be heard early in 1985.

And what about Plymouth? Who would do the campaigning there? Miss Whitaker telephoned to a number of Christian leaders in the city and in general met with the response that they could not find time to organise a campaign themselves, but would support anyone who did. It was Mrs Lumb, who in spite of much reluctance, took on the task. In the case of Plymouth a strong stand was made by a councillor, who roundly described sex shops and sex cinemas as a shame to any Christian city.

As a result of Mrs Lumb's campaign Plymouth City Council decided not to license any of the existing shops in the city. Most shops have closed, leaving one shop still open and trading without a licence. The magistrates and the firm has just been fined £1,000 and ordered to pay costs of £400. The shop has been ordered to close within 28 days.

And the rest of the West Country?

The Hon. Secretary wrote to all local authorities in Devonshire asking whether or not they had adopted powers to control the opening of sex shops and cinemas, and all replied that they had done so. She is now making similar enquiries in Somerset and Dorset.

So now there will not be any pornography on sale in the West Country? Far from it. From the shelves of most newsagents all over Devon and Cornwall magazines with filthy pictures are sold and will be sold until a reform of the Obscenity Laws makes them, as they once were, illegal.

For those of you who as groups or individuals want to tackle the problem of sex shops seriously and effectively, I have set out, by courtesy of Mr Charles Oxley, detailed advice on how this can be done (see Appendix 10).

CHAPTER 5

'None So Blind...'

Two things become very clear as one meets and talks to people; for example, during question time at public meetings. One is that people are appalled at the amount of violence in our society; the other is that they are greatly repelled by the problem. Very understandably their instinct is to 'switch off'. If there are children and young people about, that instinct is very appropriate. But if that is *all* we do then we become a part—willingly or otherwise—of one of the fundamental problems not only of the times in which we live, but of the whole of human history and experience.

Because people's instinct *is* to switch off—or to not switch on in the first place—then our reactions are likely to be both emotional and uninformed. Now please don't misunderstand me. I am not suggesting for one moment that we *should* watch violent films on television, but I am suggesting that its existence needs more than an emotional, shock-horror response—and I'm thinking here not only of physical but of verbal and emotional violence as well.

Our bodies and our minds are gifts from God. So are other people's. So are our children's. And it is against these truths that we need to assess our role in facing up to, and trying to answer, one of the most intractable problems we face—whether or not we actually possess a television set; that of the link between televised and social violence. I use the word intractable, not because I believe the problem to be insoluble, but because the forces arraigned against the finding and application of any solution are so great and so powerful. Yet, because it does so deeply affect the whole quality of our life and times (whatever the 'experts' may claim) it is up to every one of us to do what we can collectively, and individually to ensure that the arguments do not go by default. The price we, our children and our children's children will pay for any apathy on our part is beyond calculation. It is for this reason that I now set out the kind of experience and information which will, I hope, give 'grist to the mill', and provide hard facts to reinforce our emotional and instinctive concern.

It is with some sense of poignancy that I recall how, speaking on the occasion of the very first public meeting we ever held (at Birmingham Town Hall in June 5th 1964), I said 'If violence is constantly portrayed as normal on the television screen, that will help to create a violent society.' I remember also the ridicule which was directed at us for many years for even suggesting that there might be a link between social and televised violence!

No one surely is going to claim that television alone is responsible for the quite appalling increase in violent behaviour, violent language and violent crime which characterizes our society today. But most certainly we face a frightening situation which demands that we seek answers whenever and wherever they may be found.

In case we have any tendency to brush the problem aside, it's worth reminding ourselves that according to a recent Gallup Poll (in the *Daily Telegraph*, November

5th 1984), Britain is the most crime-ridden country in Europe. Personal assault ranks high amongst that crime. Surely that fact alone is more than enough to make us stop in our tracks, not only to ask why it should be so, but to see what can be done.

It is an irrefutable fact that until the arrival of commercial broadcasting, and with it the sudden proliferation of TV sets (so that now practically every home in the community possesses one) the statistics for violent crime in this country changed little since the beginning of the century.

A great deal of the new popular appeal of commercial television lay in its use of violence as a prime feature of entertainment. In 1955, the year ITV was launched, the number of crimes of violence known to the police was 7,884. By 1970 they had risen to 41,088 and by 1982 they were over 105,000. The same pattern has been seen in other countries where television relies on violence to the same degree.

The broadcasters themselves will defend any accusation of a link between television violence and real life violence by saying that the newspapers are full of tales of violence and vice, leaving little to the imagination. But television makes far more impact than the printed word; and if the old adage which says that 'One picture is worth a thousand words' is correct, how much *more* powerful is the animated, coloured, close-up picture which so often makes up the violence, whether in drama or news, that we see on our TV screens?

Take for instance the *Nine O'Clock News* on Friday, November 2nd 1984. This very understandably carried detailed coverage of the Ethiopian crisis, which has (to television's great credit) aroused enormous practical sympathy for the terrible suffering in that country.

This was followed by a story of a very different kind;

that of a Londoner who, with his wife, was awoken by
three intruders intent on stealing a sum of money. I
quote from a letter which came to us from a member of
the public.

> It was salutary to discover that the thugs were caught and
> sentenced, but intensely depressing to be told that one of
> the husband's toes was cut off and stuffed in his mouth.
> Such horror, beamed at the homes of an entire population,
> is unjustified. We feel helpless to yield assistance, and can
> only feel deeply disturbed by such reported callousness.

The same News depicted the Indian garage where a
Sikh was cornered by Hindus and burned alive. We were
also shown the face of a Sikh beaten up on a train. The lens
moved in, almost gloatingly, to record the effects of the
assault on his eye and cheek, and then on his forearm. A
generalised report without such garish touches would
have sufficed. We watch the News to be generally informed, not to be browbeaten by alarmingly grisly details.

That same programme focused on the coffin of the
Polish priest assassinated and dumped in a reservoir. This
item was not delivered via Tim Sebastian or another
reporter talking to the camera, but through glimpses of
distraught mourners grieving over the butchered church-
man. Emotional tension was high in a certain part of
Warsaw; and we saw it with stunning clarity.

Next came the Iraq–Iran War. No cool account was
given of recent developments. Instead we were submitted
to a treatment which would not have disgraced the pages
of 'Boys Own' magazine. Our reporter was in the thick of
it. We saw the dust, the dirt, 'a fountain of blood', a
tracheotomised throat. (Does Graham Bright's Bill cover
this form of 'video nasty'?) Rocket launchers blasted away
merrily. The grim awfulness of these accumulated reports
had, by now, thoroughly sickened and alarmed myself
and my family—and, I surmise, countless others.

There was the slim counterbalance of a heart transplant
patient doing well, but again we almost witnessed tears
(this time, admittedly, of gratitude) as his mother talked

of the donor's parents. Real tears were evinced in the same lurid News with the story of an old soldier brought from Canada and honoured for his valour so many years ago. He—wait for it—broke down and wept.

All this, compounded by the continuing saga of the miners' strike, made for some of the most compulsively dire viewing one could wish for—compulsive in the same way as 'Psycho' is compulsive, or 'Star Wars', or a soap opera. One's critical faculties were left a long way behind. The information supremos were aiming at the lachrymal glands, and coaxing a lump in one's throat or the rising of one's gorge. The targeting was successful, but it was a programme the BBC should be ashamed of—not because of what was portrayed, but because of the way in which it was portrayed.

I almost forgot the Granny who was executed in the States by injection after a protracted spell on Death Row. I can only feel that a scoop was missed here in that her nearest and dearest were not observed breaking down hysterically. Thankfully, the authorities did not allow us to observe the needle enter the skin, the plunger of the syringe depressed with macabre thoroughness, for if they had we should surely have seen it, courtesy of The Nine O'Clock News.

Of course all that was news, and important news; but it does raise the issue of whether that 'fact' is the beginning and end of the decision to create a news bulletin of such unrelieved gloom. Is consideration given to the impact it will collectively have in terms of depression, hopelessness and desensitivity?

Looking back now at the events which surrounded the riots in Toxteth and Brixton in 1981 I am amazed—and by no means for the first time—at how I almost missed that 'still small voice' which on so many occasions has inspired some initiative that turned out to be far more significant than one could ever have realized at the time.

On the night of Friday 10th July 1981, countless numbers of people sat and watched the coverage on ITN of the riots then taking place in Toxteth on the outskirts of Liverpool. There was one sequence in particular which is as vivid in my mind now as it was on the night it happened. I remember commenting to my husband, 'Well, if ever there was a case of teaching the techniques of violence, that was it!'

What had we just seen?

A couple of coloured youths were shown walking in a perfectly innocuous manner along a peaceful pavement in Toxteth (the very fact that they were seen doing so meant that the TV camera was already in position and operating). Suddenly, as they passed a gentlemen's outfitters one of them, with no apparent incitement of any kind, violently kicked out at the huge plate glass window. The youths sprang back as the window crashed down in pieces on to the pavement (useful tip to pick up there!) and then, after a moment or two to allow it to settle, stepped across the pile of glass to help themselves to the clothes now available to any looter—including themselves! I still have a vivid picture in my mind of one of the youths holding a jacket against his body to see if it would fit before slinging it over his arms, along with anything else he could quickly grab. His pal did likewise.

We were appalled; as indeed, it turned out, were most people. But our first reaction was to feel that in a situation of such national significance, anything *we* might do would be lost in the general mayhem. However, we decided that whether our complaint was noted or not we had to make our Association's reactions known. We sent two telegrams, one to Peter Woon, editor of BBC Television News (who had also covered the story) and one to David Nicholas, editor of Independent Television News. Both telegrams urged,

'Please consider whether the current massive television coverage of acts of vandalism and violence is contributing to the spread of the riots....'

To our utter amazement both TV news channels carried the story—the ITN going as far as to show a photograph of the telegram itself! Which really *did* underline for me the importance of obeying 'the whisper'.

It should be said that they responded to our complaint in a way which was both honest and responsible—and, I think it should be added, quite unusually so. David Nicholas admitted that 'Media coverage of the disturbance last week has probably had some copycat effect'. Peter Woon joined him by saying, 'It would be foolish to pretend that there has been no copycat effect.' Very wide concern was expressed, not least in Parliament, about the role of television in teaching the techniques of violent protest. *The Times* (August 10th 1981) had this to say:

> First we should ask ourselves: Can anyone seriously doubt there was a strong copycat element in the riots?.... That many youths wore balaclavas or plastic bags over their heads? That there was a rash of fires in dustbins? Or that so many milk floats were commandeered? How else do you explain the spread of this behaviour? Was it by word of mouth from Toxteth to Wood Green? Was it over the telephone? Scarcely a medium of mass communication!

So great was the concern over the violence in Toxteth, and later in Brixton, that the Government set up an Enquiry under Lord Scarman. In his report (*The Brixton Disorders 1981*) Lord Scarman had this to say.

> The Media, particularly the Broadcasting Media, do in my view bear a responsibility for the escalation of the

disorders (including the looting) in Brixton on Saturday 11 April and for their continuation the following day, and for the imitative element in the later disorders elsewhere....I do urge editors and producers...at all times to bear in mind that rioters, and others, in their exhibition of violence respond alarmingly to what they see (wrongly but understandably) as the encouraging presence of the TV camera and the reporter. [In his conclusion Lord Scarman emphasized particularly, and as a matter of urgency,] the need for Newspaper Editors, Television and Radio producers, and Journalists to give continuous attention to the social implications of their awesome power to influence the minds, the attitudes and the behaviour, not only of the reading, viewing and listening public, but also of those whose unlawful behaviour they report.

But what was the considered response of the broadcasting industry? A very revealing account of events by David Cox, Head of Current Affairs at London Weekend, appeared in *Television Today* (April 22nd 1982).

He said that Stephen Hearst, controller of the BBC Future Policy Group—one of the 'executives primed to take action in defence of their industry's image' —happened to 'run into' Dr Michael Tracey, head of the British Film Institute's new Broadcasting Research Unit, who was 'seeking targets for probes of topicality and relevance'. And 'by the time the cheeseboard had arrived, a project of apparent mutual benefit had been devised' according to the article. And what was that project?

In almost no time at all Mr Howard Tumber, working for the BFI research unit, had completed a report entitled *Television and the Riots* which attempted to answer the question whether some of the rioting had been caused by copycat effect induced by television.

The Report was financed by the BBC and the IBA with what was, considering the importance of the subject, quite a trifling sum—something like £1,000. It effectively rejected Lord Scarman's conclusions and took no account whatever of the long-term conditioning effect of televised violence, nor of the cumulative effect of the coverage of techniques of violent protest— stoning, burning of cars, petrol bombs, etc.—which have appeared on our television screens for many years. The youngsters of Toxteth, as elsewhere, have grown up with violence as a normal concomitant of life, and to deny that it could in certain special circumstances trigger off violent reaction is to live in a very unreal world indeed.

There is something very disturbing about the speed and alacrity with which the BBC and IBA jump to defend themselves, and something quite frightening about the way in which they try to wear down challenge —particularly in this field of violence, from whatever source it may come—to the lack of social and intellectual integrity which characterizes official policies within both Authorities. To dismiss, with coolness and aplomb, as the Broadcasting Authorities do, the power of the animated, verbal, brilliantly coloured picture to affect thinking and therefore, inevitably, behaviour is, if taken to its logical conclusion, to deny the power of the spoken and the printed word. Indeed, it is to render every aspect of communication meaningless.

One last word on the subject of 'copycat' effects. Perhaps you, like me, smiled wryly at the report published about the same time that the Broadcasting Authorities were taking very seriously the concern expressed by a Community Health Council in the West Midlands about close-ups on television of footballers spitting on the field. The Council believe that youngsters copying their football heroes could spread TB. There is no sign here of research into the effect of televised spitting on social behaviour. The BBC 'deplore it' and claim to make every effort not to show it. One can't help but wish that some BBC spokesman would tell us why youngsters copy spitting, but apparently don't copy anything else!

At the end of this chapter it is perhaps worth casting our minds back to the beginning of it—namely, to the 'still small voice' that prompted us to telephone. Not because we want to emphasize, in this case, our success; but to reinforce the extraordinary benefit which can result from picking up a telephone and refusing to think that what we, individually do, can have no effect.

CHAPTER 6

'There Can Be No Defence...'

In the light of massive and continuing public concern such as we have been describing, one was first startled, then dismayed and deeply disappointed at the attitude now being adopted by, in particular, Mr John Whitney, Director General of the IBA. Dismissing the conviction held by the Metropolitan Police that the rise in crime is linked with television, similarly discounting the concern expressed by both Labour and Conservative Home Secretaries about the role of television in increasing our problems associated with the maintenance of law and order, and making no reference whatsoever to the fact that ITV is dependant upon the power of television to affect people's response to TV advertising, Mr Whitney claims that 'It is true that after thirty years of television in Britain there is *no evidence* that it makes ordinary kids into violent kids nor that it bears responsibility for national crime rates'. But no one *is* saying that television is responsible for national crime rates. What we *are* saying is that it carries a heavy responsibility which it would appear, if Mr Whitney has his way, the authority he represents will never face up to in the imaginative and constructive fashion which is so desperately needed.

A posture of defensiveness—surely born of pride—in

the face of our growing culture of violence and all that that means in every area of our national life, is itself indefensible. When members of a broadcasting authority are themselves, as individuals, pleasant and responsible people, it is more than sad that collectively they seem hooked upon the drug of violence ratings.

Mr Whitney also revived the idea that watching violence on television would make people less violent. But the claim that such violence could have a cathartic effect was hawked around in the sixties and early seventies by those (particularly in the USA) who had a commercial interest in the sale of cheaply made TV films often based entirely on violence of one kind or another—verbal and physical. It fills one with dismay to find someone in Mr Whitney's position reviving it as a self-justification.

The catharsis theory has been discredited by many leading psychiatrists. For example Dr Wertham, consultant psychiatrist and senior psychiatrist at Bellevue Hospital, New York, said, 'This outlet theory is not only overdone: it is false. It is pseudo-scientific dogma. There is no shred of clinical evidence for it. On the contrary, the children are over-excited without being given adequate release. Delinquent behaviour is not prevented but promoted.'

On another level there is this fascinating quote from a book[1] by G. H. Hendrick in which we are given the results of a survey conducted by a prisoner in a maximum security prison in Michigan, USA.

He interviewed 208 of the 688 prisoners at Marquette Jail, Michigan, and asked their views on the relationship between crime and violence on TV and that in real life.

[1] G. H. Hendrick, *When Television is a School for Criminals* (1977).

Ninety percent claimed they had actually learned new tricks and improved their criminal expertise by watching crime programmes. Forty percent said they had attempted specific crimes they saw on TV, though only about one-third of these attempts were successful. Most of the prisoners have a personal TV set in their cells. A 34 year old man with 15 years jail behind him said, 'TV has taught me how to steal cars, how to break into establishments, how to go about robbing people, even how to roll a drunk.' Currently in jail serving a sentence for rape, he said, 'Nowadays I watch TV in my cell from 4.00 pm until midnight. I just sit back and take notes.'

Still in America the US Surgeon General and the National Institute for Mental Health concluded, in 1982, that the evidence that television violence has a harmful effect on normal viewers was 'overwhelming' while the US Department of Justice has concluded (1983) that virtually 100% of aggression researchers agree that there is a cause-effect relationship between the consumption of entertainment violence and an increased tendency towards anger and violence in viewers. The US Attorney General's Task Force on Family Violence reported early in 1984 that the evidence is becoming 'overwhelming' that television violence is a significant factor in the high levels of violence in the American family.

And for good measure I will quote Michael Rothenberg M.D., writing as long ago as 1975 in the *Journal of the American Medical Association*:

One hundred and forty-six articles in behavioural science journals, representing 50 studies involving 10,000 children and adolescents from every conceivable background, all showed that violence viewing produced increased aggressive behaviour in the young and that immediate remedial action in terms of television programming is warranted.

It is shameful—how can one describe it otherwise?—that, with all their stream of 'investigative' programmes of one kind or another no broadcasting authority is prepared to inform its viewers, and indeed society as a whole, of the proven harm of violent entertainment. And it is against the background of widespread and continuing academic evidence of this kind that Mr John Whitney's claim of 'no evidence' appears culpably naive, to say the least. It is also sad that his comments were made at a time when concern is growing in the public mind about the threats posed by our increasingly violent society, and what part the reporting of violent news as well as violent entertainment is playing in it all.

The concern is not just whether violence breeds actual violence, but with its effect upon the whole personality. It may well have been the dubious reaction of the news editor of one of our national newspapers to John Whitney's remarks that resulted in a report about the effects of a 'video nasty' upon an eight-year old boy being printed alongside his report.

According to the other report, the boy was so affected after watching a particularly unpleasant 'nasty' that he had to be referred for clinical treatment. He had been invited by a classmate to go to his house to see 'this smashing video Dad bought home'. Dr Elizabeth Newson, director of the Child Development Research Unit at Nottingham University, told John Izbicki, Education Correspondent of the *Daily Telegraph*,

> This young boy watched a highly questionable and violent video film for only 20 minutes and was totally shattered and disabled by the experience. He simply could no longer control his own thoughts about it and suffered recurring nightmares.... The unit has now had its first referrals from schools of youngsters suffering states of extreme anxiety as a result of watching video nasties.

Apparently psychiatrists throughout the country have become so concerned about the growing number of young patients with 'video nasty symptoms' that the Royal College of Psychiatry has given the go-ahead for a nationwide survey. Questionnaires have been sent to psychiatrists asking for consulting room case histories, and their connection, if any, with sex and violence on television or video.

One awaits the results of those questionnaires with some considerable interest. One wonders also whether the IBA will still be able to so smugly dismiss concern about the impact of sex and violence on television.

Let me say at once that as I write in 1984 there does seem to be, at least as far as the BBC is concerned, a marked decrease in the use of violence during 'family viewing time' (up to nine o'clock in the evening), though the late night films on both channels often tell a very different story. However, it could be argued that while a decrease in violence on television is much to be welcomed, it has come almost too late. One thing is certain. The violence, often crude and gratuitous, violates the guidelines issued to producers by both the BBC and the IBA.

The BBC's guidelines on the treatment of violence (*The Portrayal of Violence in Television Programmes*) were first published in 1972 (see Appendix 6), and although updated from time to time remain much the same. The contrast between what is *supposed* to happen and what actually does happen is quite startling. The Corporation tells its producers:

> In programmes for adult audiences, no less care should be taken than in children's programmes to avoid providing examples of weapons ready to hand or of tactics to use in fistfights. Violence ought not to be presented in ways

which might glorify it or portray it as a proper solution to interpersonal conflicts. It is particularly important that 'good' characters should not perform actions which might appear cruel to the child audience, however honourable the intentions of the 'good' characters may be....Even when violence forms a legitimate element in a production, the manner in which it is presented must be carefully thought about....Any attempt to make violence an essential characteristic of manliness, for example, should be avoided. Violence as an inevitable solution to a fictional situation should only be invoked in relatively rare instances....Avoid setting examples which can easily be copied such as the use of knives or broken bottles in fights, nooses, trip-wires, karate chops, or the locking-up of 'prisoners' in outhouses, empty rooms or cellars.

As far as news bulletins are concerned, producers are told:

> The violence of the events should never be sensationalised and should always be put into the perspective of the rest of the world's news of the day. Dead bodies should not be shown in close-up and film should not dwell on close-up pictures of the grief-stricken and suffering in the wake of natural disasters or man-made violence. The presence of a film camera can itself incite violence and some partisan groups and exhibitionist hooligans are keen to snatch any opportunity to achieve a wider audience for their activities. The use of cameras should be as inconspicuous as possible and coverage of violence or vandalism in crowds at football matches or other sports events should be kept to a minimum.

Equally, the IBA makes clear at least its *official* position, even though this does not always work out in practice!

> There can be no defence of violence shown solely for its own sake, or of the gratuitous exploitation of sadistic or

other perverted practices. Violence, menace and threats can take many forms—emotional, physical and verbal. Scenes of domestic friction, whether or not accompanied by physical violence, can easily cause fear and insecurity....The Working Party is convinced that there is no alternative to a continuing assumption that the portrayal of violence may have harmful effects. Research has shown that it is dangerous to assume that depiction of the use of violence for legitimate ends is less harmful than depiction of violence for evil ends.[Producers are warned against] ingenious and unfamiliar methods of inflicting pain or injury...

No doubt my readers will come to their own conclusions about how seriously such instructions are taken by those responsible for programmes.

Thinking about violence, and the images we have seen on our television screen during the Miners' Strike of 1984, I turned again to some research we carried out in 1978 which looked specifically at the treatment of the police in two widely viewed programmes at that time. I could not help but wonder, as I re-read it, just what part such programmes had played in the conditioning of the attitudes of the young in particular—but by no means solely—to the police at this time.

We called our report *LAW—and Disorder*.

This piece of research has been carried out by the National VALA at a time of rising violent and non-violent crime; when an undermanned police force is working often under conditions of very considerable personal risk, and in a climate soured by anti-police propaganda of a political nature.

National VALA appreciates that the job the police and Special Branch officers, in particular, have to perform will bring them into constant contact with much that is vicious, dirty and sordid. However, in the name of 'reality' viewers are subjected to the foulest language and the most vicious of violence as well as the endless sexual exploits of the main characters in these programmes.

We realize that policemen are perfectly capable, upon occasion, of using bad language, losing their tempers, and behaving in a manner which is less than responsible. We do *not* accept that police officers, as a matter of course, are foul-mouthed, sadistically violent and promiscuous.

We fully accept that programmes which show confrontation between criminals and the police will, upon occasion, contain violence. We do not accept that such violence has to be sadistic, nor that programmes should demonstrate that criminals are only apprehended by violent means.

We believe that the programmes 'The Sweeney' and 'Target' have helped to undermine public confidence in the police at a time of considerable social and political stress. And that this is indefensible.

Furthermore, we understand that these programmes have been sold abroad—in the case of 'The Sweeney', already 'Worldwide' [Thames TV spokesman]. On the assumption that our contention is correct that these programmes are damaging to the image of the police force in this country, how damaging they must also be to the image of Britain abroad.

The Broadcasting Authorities have a duty to serve the public interest. The upholding of police morale and public confidence in the Police Force should be, in the Association's view, of paramount importance to both the BBC and the IBA. This is not to say that police officers should be portrayed as more than human, it is to say that they should not be portrayed as so immoral a profession as to breed contempt amongst the public as a whole, or, it should also be said, as to embarrass, or disquiet, the families of serving officers, particularly the young wives.

The persistent theme of these two programmes, often reinforced by good acting and production and brilliant camera work, has been that the end always justifies the means, and that those whose job it is to uphold law and order are as corrupt as those who defy it. Such a theme is untrue and mischievous. Its effect is destructive of public trust and security.

The obscene and blasphemous language used in these two programmes came as much from the police as the criminals; the often sadistic violence was practised as much by the police as by the criminals; promiscuity was, in fact, much more a characteristic of the police than of the criminals. In other words, there was little, if anything to choose between them.

Repeated kicking in the groin, vicious punching in the stomach are by no means uncommon practice by the police officers in these programmes. Since such behaviour is known to cause serious injury this is totally unacceptable. In the light of research which shows an undoubted link between television violence and real life violence such incidents are criminally irresponsible.

I have no wish to overburden my readers with too many disturbing images, but I hope they will accept the need to illustrate my point with one example from each channel.

Firstly, from the BBC's 'Target': Chief Superintendent Hackett involved in a fight with criminal; feet used brutally by both parties; Hackett ends up with a knife at criminal's throat. He is pulled away by colleague. Kicks criminal into the sea after having had his foot on his throat. (Hackett declares—'I'll find him, even if I have to live up his backside for a month.')

Secondly, from 'The Sweeney': Police officer chases criminal downstairs, traps him at bottom and delivers vicious punch after vicious punch at the bleeding face and head of a now helpless man. Has to be pulled away by colleague. In the middle of a fight to arrest a criminal, a detective punches a woman straight in the face. A second woman pulled violently to the ground by another police officer.

Add to all this violence foul and coarse language and the contempt for and sexual exploitation of women which characterized this series, and I think it must be conceded that these factors carry some responsibility for the decrease in respect for the police which is now typical of our society.

Even John Alderson, formerly Chief Constable of Devon and Cornwall and noted for his 'liberal' attitudes, had this to say in his book *Policing Freedom*:

> The police are ill served by television… television series are capable of undermining public confidence in the police and the self confidence of the police themselves…. The police are vulnerable to damage from television unless corrective measures are taken.

So, indeed, are we all; and the violence on television must of course be seen as only one part, albeit a very important part, of the whole of our culture of violence and we need to be particularly aware of the exploitation of the young by the violence in videos and in rock music.

It is not my purpose in writing this book to shock my readers to the extent that they abandon all hope of constructive action, but perhaps the following synopsis of just one of the many violent rock videos available will demonstrate how vital it is that we keep an eye—and an ear—on the type of material our children are watching. We all know the temptation to pack the youngsters off into their own rooms to give us a bit of peace!

> 'Hero' grabbed and kidnapped. Police hit man with club. Man executed with bag over head. 'Hero' drives car into a church full of 'bad guys'. Everyone goes mad with automatic pistols and machine guns etc.

I think we need too to realize the significance of the 'heavy metal' image with its studded belts, wrist-bands, rings, knuckle dusters, barb-wire necklaces, and the T-shirts with violent images and messages.

Of course, many young people just think of such 'hardware' as fun, but it is really very important that as parents and teachers and youth leaders we discuss the deeper significance of such gear. After all, if we become accustomed to think of such a style and indeed for that matter the presentation of violence in the media as 'fun' is there not a danger that our reaction to real violence may be diminished, and even that a few of us may get to the place where we can hardly differentiate between reality and fantasy?

CHAPTER 7

'Just a Matter of Taste?'

In 1969 we fought successfully against the publication and distribution in Britain of the subversive *Little Red School Book*. In 1972 the one and a half million signatures collected by National VALA and the then Festival of Light on the Nationwide Petition for Public Decency resulted in the first Indecent Displays Bill. This was introduced, as a private member's bill, by Mr Tim Sainsbury, M.P. Although it was 1981 before such a law was on the Statute Book, it has had considerable effect in 'cleaning up' the bookshelves. In 1978 Mr Cyril Townsend's private member's bill resulted in the Protection of Children Act which made child pornography illegal. Then there was the successful private prosecution against a blasphemous poem in *Gay News*. This case re-established the blasphemy law as still effective, even though the last previous case was heard in 1922. And, of course, there has been the much more recent campaign against 'video nasties' which resulted in the Video Recordings Act of 1984. Throughout all this time we have seen the need for a tightening up of the obscenity law. At the time of writing, that is our priority. If this particular campaign is successful, then such a law will, without in any way being repressive, make the most important contribution of all to the fight to uphold decency as the vast majority of people see it.

Even as I write I am very conscious of the fact that the word 'censorship' may already be in the reader's mind, raising doubts and questions. It is, I think, worth recording that the campaign to link our work with censorship was launched by the activists of the 'anti-censorship-at-all-costs' lobby as a reaction to the highly successful campaign being waged by our 'Clean Up TV' initiative in the 1960s.

The pornographers, supported by those who wanted total licence rather than responsible control within the media, were given enormous and continuous coverage in the media and particularly on television. At the same time we were ridiculed, misrepresented and 'banned'! I was officially censored off BBC television for eleven years (a state of affairs, I am happy to say, which has long passed).

One of the cleverest slogans of the libertarian brigade was that everything was 'all a matter of personal taste'. That concept has sunk very deeply into our national consciousness. The self-interest and abdication of responsibility that lies behind it has been disguised by shouts of 'freedom'. But in truth, the publication of pernicious, immoral and obscene material on television, in magazines, books and films, and in the theatre has been destructive of the very concept of freedom in its truest sense.

Take the matter of *The Little Red School Book*. This was obviously aimed at school children and was published by an international revolutionary group. In court, the publisher Richard Handyside stated that it was intended for children of eleven and over. It contained such advice as 'There ought to be one or several contraceptive machines in every school.... Porn is a harmless pleasure if it isn't taken seriously...you may get some good ideas from it and find something that you haven't tried before.' The fact that children were invited to write for advice and information to various bodies listed in the extremist revolutionary *Agitprop Directory* underlines how often sexual and political revolution go hand in hand.

The book was found to be obscene and confiscated in 1971, and this verdict was upheld on appeal in this country, and in the European Court of Justice. Nevertheless it was widely circulated by humanist and revolutionary bodies in Britain, and it must have had some effect on many of those who were children then but are adults now.

Soon after the *Little Red School Book* trial came the longest obscenity trial in legal history, lasting twenty-six days—that of the publishers of *The School Kids OZ!* This resulted in sentences ranging from nine to fifteen months which provoked unprecedented fury amongst the hippies waiting outside the court, and led to a kerbside battle between the police and the furious *OZ* supporters. These sentences were suspended and reduced on appeal due to 'a serious misdirection of the jury'. The trial gave rise to a tremendous wave of support for the defendants by the Press and television, the tabling of a Commons motion by eleven Labour M.P.s (which presented these men as victims of an 'oppressive right wing judiciary') and a predictable outcry from the National Council for Civil Liberties.

It is difficult now, fourteen years on, for those not actively involved to remember what these trials were all about. In essence what we were witnessing was not just an attack upon childhood itself, but a calculated campaign to involve even very young children in a way of life which was highly politicized and anarchic. One of the most disturbing elements of both the *Little Red School Book* case and the *OZ* trial was the lack of any compassion or imaginative understanding of the child himself. Indeed one could go further and condemn without reservation the callous exploitation of the child for political purposes.

It is immensely important that we do realize the link between sexual anarchy—do as you please when you please, no matter who gets hurt—and political anarchy, elements of which we see at work in our own society today.

This was something which I certainly did not understand when we started campaigning on what seemed the simple issue of 'cleaning-up television' in the early sixties. But I have come to understand that the destruction of character and family life which is the inevitable consequence of a sexual 'free-for-all' leads inevitably to political anarchy, the destruction of our culture and our democratic way of life. Most important of all, it undercuts the very foundation of our Christian faith.

When that happens, a society either disintegrates or it is taken over by a dictatorship of the left or the right. A letter in the *Sunday Times* (August 9th 1970) and an event in the United States vividly illustrated the dangers facing a society which 'goes soft'. The letter drew attention to a passage from *Cinema Documents*, a publication produced under the supervision of the Italian Communist Party, on what should be the right attitude to sex shows. The passage reads:

> We are interested in encouraging this type of play, and we are likewise prepared to praise actors of such plays as champions of artistic freedom. We want to encourage this sort of artistic production, and must lead people on to

produce others that are, sexually speaking, more daring still, and that contain scenes that are downright scandalous.

As a tactical policy, our aim is to defend an enterprise that is pornographic and entirely free from the restrictions of ordinary moral rules. They (directors and actors) are in effect like ants working voluntarily and without pay for us as they eat away at the very roots of their bourgeois society. Why should we stop them from their work? Why should we place obstacles in their path?

Perhaps even more telling are the following extracts from *The Naked Communist* by W. Cleon Skousen, which were placed in the United States Congressional Record for June 10th 1963. Skousen worked for the American Federal Bureau of Investigation and spent twelve years on the waterfronts of the great American ports studying the techniques of communist infiltration and tactics in a free society. Altogether forty objectives were listed by Skousen, but the following are particularly relevant to this argument.

1. Break down cultural standards of morality by promoting pornography and obscenity in books, magazines, motion pictures, radio and television.
2. Eliminate all laws governing obscenity by calling them 'censorship' and a violation of free speech and free press.
3. Gain control of key positions in radio, television and motion pictures.
4. Discredit the family as an institution. Encourage promiscuity and easy divorce.
5. Emphasize the need to raise children away from the negative influence of parents. Attribute prejudice, mental blocks and retarding of children to the suppressive influence of parents.
6. Present homosexuality, degeneracy and promiscuity

as 'normal, natural and healthy'.

7. Continue discrediting culture by degrading all forms of artistic expression.
8. Infiltrate the churches and replace revealed religion with 'social' religion. Discredit the Bible and emphasize the need for intellectual maturity which does not need a 'religious crutch'.
9. Eliminate prayer or any phase of religious expression from schools.
10. Create the impression that violence and insurrection are legitimate aspects of the country's tradition, that students and special-interest groups should rise up and use force to solve economic, political and social problems.

I would not for a moment suggest that all those who support greater permissiveness in the arts, who appear more concerned to support a 'social' than a biblical emphasis within the church are left wing activists. But I think, nonetheless, we are called to be 'as wise as serpents' as well as 'gentle as doves', and we do no service to our cause if we are naive or if we find such insights into the works of the devil in our own day too frightening to face.

For myself, each time I read the above extract from Cleon Skousens' book I am struck not by any sense of outdatedness—it is after all more than twenty years since the objectives were published—but by a sickness at the pit of my stomach. They grow more topical year by year.

We have come to understand, too, how very relevant it is to realize the historical attitude, for example, of the far right of Nazism, as well as the far left of International Communism to the problem we now have to combat. Such understanding does surely destroy, once and for all, the justification that pornography is 'all a matter of personal taste', and that what one decides to buy and what one watches in one's own home is no one else's business.

It was in 1980 that Count Nikolai Tolstoy, the historian and descendant of the great Russian writer Leo Tolstoy, addressed the National VALA Convention. What he had to say was of enormous interest to us all, and remains increasingly relevant to us; not least because it is clear how, even in the five years since, some of his fears and predictions have come to pass.

Now those opposed to control are very difficult to pin down—what the trendies hold in one decade they will have abandoned by the next. 30 years ago liberal writers were saying that their ideas would not spread to abuse children, to encourage sadistic trends, to public display, to pornography in shop windows. Ten years later they have modified that statement and it seems to me that they will slither and slide down the slope wherever it leads them. Some people now say that it's quite harmless and won't lead to sexual crime because people would sublimate their own desires by reading about them. As I see it, it won't be long before they move on to what all this literature and TV is tending towards—at the moment the violence and cruelty is confined to simulation, but it won't be for ever.

History shows the pattern of progress—eventually it was real blood in the Roman circuses that the crowds were after. Audiences no longer appreciated gladiatorial skill etc—if there was no blood they howled for a new act.... That's what we shall see here.

At present most of the pornographers agree that what is right for adults is not right for children. I suspect that we shall see that age limit slipping lower and lower. Amongst the pornography supporters I detect a strident note that they object to any who in their own homes still resist all this...the day may not be far off when you cannot even escape in your own homes. This is an area where my historical interests have often directed me....

The whole of civilised society is based on subtle relationships of trust, faith and honour between people...a central theme of all Shakespeare's plays is the essential upholding of honour and trust between people...when this breaks down there is appalling bloodshed, chaos and destruction.

Germany's Weimar Republic (1919–33) was just the sort of society which most of us are trying to prevent arriving here. A distinguished historian of that period says of the pre-Nazi German Republic: 'Morality came to be divorced from sexual matters and in Berlin all manner of sexual licence and aberrations could be indulged without shame or restraint. Virginity lost its esteem and contraceptive practices gained official recognition. Nudism, homosexuality, sadism, masochism flaunted themselves with immoderation that shocked visitors from Latin countries. The repulsive licence of republican Germany was a preparation for the callous immorality indoctrinated by the Nazi creed. The ascendance of cruelty had begun.

The Brownshirt movement (over 1m. strong when Hitler came to power) was led by the chief of staff Ernst Röhm, a practising homosexual. Nearly all Brownshirt leaders were part of a ring of homosexuals...this was drawn to Hitler's attention, but as he said the Nazi movement was not a training ground for high school girls.

Hitler himself would not have disapproved of the tendencies we see in England today. I quote from someone who knew him for many years before breaking with him and escaping from him before the war broke out.... 'Hitler had a room with obscene nudes on the wall concealing nothing. Such pictures have no artistic intention or appeal. He revels in this style of painting...and keeps by his bed pornographic magazines to read in privacy.'

It's an odd coincidence that a high official of the Soviet political police who defected to the West learned from officers of the Kremlin guard that Stalin too delighted in pornography which he kept in secret by his bed.

In Nazi Germany the epitome of all pornography was Streicher's *Der Sturmer* newspaper which Hitler described as Germany's respectable form of pornography. Under the guise of attacking Jews and Roman Catholics there were graphic descriptions and illustrations of hideous sexual crimes supposedly committed by Jews and nuns. Some of Hitler's staff complained about it but Hitler himself always protected Streicher and his newspaper.

Most pornography of course is hostile to women, presents women in degrading positions and much of it of course goes in for actual cruelty.

It's not without significance that much of this pornography deals in Nazi symbolism—jackbooted men with swastika armbands whipping women—all this not very far beneath the surface.

If we are to preserve ourselves from such a society—and I don't think it's alarmist when you look at the shortlived Weimar Republic and how logically the Nazis extended the violence and cruelty permeated in the thought of that society and used it to their own ends.

Much the same happened in the destruction of the old Russian society. These trains of thought are of course part of the spirit of the times—they're not consciously worked out. There are documents, some genuine which show that the KGB was implicated in spreading pornography in an attempt to dissolve the links of family life and personal loyalties.... Today the KGB fully recognises the danger of the family unit, of religion and other non-state, non-totalitarian standards and ethics.

One of the horrifying aspects of the Gulag camps (which at their peak in 1945 probably had some 20m. inhabitants working on forced labour) was the fact that the moment people were deported to these camps the men were instantly separated from their families. I quote from Russian orders captured by Germans in 1941 issued by Deputy Commissar Shirov 4-6-41 about deportation of Balts from their occupied lands: 'In view of the fact that a large number of deportees must be arrested and distributed in special camps...it is essential that the operation of removal of the deportee's family and its head should be carried out simultaneously without notifying them of the separation confronting them.'

So even in the camps, far from any civilised life and guarded by a million NKVD guards, the Soviet state still felt threatened in its authority by the mere existence of husbands, wives and children together. I think it's on behalf of families as much as anything else that I hope we will go out from this gathering and continue our struggle.

CHAPTER 8

The Schoomaster in the Lions' Den

Meeting him for the first time it is hard to imagine anyone less likely than Charles Oxley, M.A., Vice President, National VALA, becoming involved with the group PIE (Paedophile Information Exchange) which advocates sex with children (see Appendix 7). He is a tall, humorous, bespectacled, successful academic, principal of several Christian schools—two in Liverpool and one near Glasgow—with a combined attendance of over 2,000 children.

Such is his great concern for all children that he started an extremely hazardous mission which put at risk both his professional and personal reputation—he joined the highly secretive paedophile society as a spy! His involvement with the organization began when he was sent a cutting about their activities which angered and sickened him on a most profound level, and made him determined to do everything possible to destroy the movement. He also wrote an article attacking PIE and that drew a reply from a Mr Tom O'Carroll who was then a publicity officer with the Open University. Charles recalls how the letter was signed 'Yours sinfully, p.p. Satan'! However, the letter also contained a Post Office box number, and it took only a moment for Charles to realize that this gave him the opportunity he sought. So he wrote to O'Carroll, signing his letter 'Dave Charlton', and told him that he would like to know more about his organization. His real purpose was to gain access to the code names and false addresses behind which members of PIE hid, and hand them over to the police.

Without being in any way under instruction from the police he sifted through all the PIE literature, met senior officials and attended committee meetings. All this started seven years ago and we who know Charles so well as a person appreciated something of the extreme risks he took and were amazed at his courage and dedication.

Time and again during these years Charles left his schools to drive down to London where the PIE meetings took place. So great was his determination to get the maximum information about their activities that he set about gaining their confidence in every possible way. Charles has spoken since of his wife's apprehension but also of how she recognized that PIE was an evil thing that had to be stopped. He has also admitted that he knew very well that, as a teacher, his involvement could expose him to very great danger and misinterpretation of his motives. Because he realized that his plan could go very badly wrong, one of the first things he did was to make contact with the Vice Squad at New Scotland Yard. He kept one officer there informed of all developments as they transpired.

The correspondence which now began with PIE was to last for seven years and Charles arranged for this mail to be sent not to the school but to the home of an elderly relative. She was given strict instructions never to open it.

Charles has said since 'I hated reading their publications. We cannot deal with filthy men without expecting a little of the filth to stick to one's own hands.'

However, as time went on Charles came to realize that more than correspondence was needed if he was ever to bring this group to book. So in 1981 he decided that he would have a better chance of fighting PIE from inside. 'When it came to the crunch whether I should join or let the matter drop, joining was the lesser of two evils,' he said. 'It's the children, you see. I am 61 and schoolmastering has been my life…looking after children, caring for children, giving them moral values as well as good education. So people like this must be my natural enemies.'

So now 'Dave Charlton' periodically forsook his headmasterly garb, dressed casually in an opennecked shirt and drove to the PIE committee meetings, hiding his car in side roads in case his registration number might be traced. He speaks of how he drove down to those meetings in 'shabby terraced houses in east and north London' and he tells of how glad he was of the long drives home—'the clean air was very therapeutic.'

In order to get as much inside information as he possibly could, Charles offered to type and help edit articles for the organization's magazine. 'I was planning all the time to get my hands on their mailing list and I offered the use of my word processor to them. They were very pleased with that!'

Charles speaks of his experiences with a mixture of humour and distaste. He made 'good progress' on the committee. 'I often couldn't quite believe where I was! At my first full meeting I was greeted by a failed boxer with a dyed blond crew cut, a dirty teeshirt and very short satin blue shorts and nothing else on. The room we were in was smoke-filled and shabby. A vicar's son was lolling on a broken settee reading a pornographic magazine.'

At the very last meeting he attended, Charles saw the membership mailing list put into a sports bag with proofs of the latest issue of an obscene magazine. It was taken off to work by a member of the committee who was on a double shift as a security guard at the Home Office. This man, Steven Smith, fled to Holland after having been committed for trial at the Old Bailey; at the time of writing the Dutch police are unwilling to extradite him.

It was this extraordinary and committed dedication on the part of Charles Oxley that played a crucial role in the police prosecution against the paedophiles, David Joy and Peter Bremner. In the event both men were cleared by an all-male jury at the Old Bailey on November 13th 1984 of four charges of incitement to commit sexual offences against children. But both men were unanimously found guilty of charges under the Post Office Act (see Appendix 8). David Joy—also convicted for publishing an obscene article—was jailed for eighteen months, and Peter Bremner for six months. Sentencing them Judge John Owen, Q.C., said: 'I bear in mind that emotion is a poor judge in matters of fact. I shall do my best to curb my emotions. In sentencing you I must not let my revulsion at the contents of this magazine affect me more than is proper.' He went on 'The law is designed to protect children from such people and one of the most dangerous aspects of your organization was that it sought to give an intellectual respectability to acts which society as a whole regards as loathsome.'

Naturally there was tremendous Press and public interest and concern over this case, which brought to the forefront of public attention an evil which tended to lie outside the knowledge of the average person, except in perhaps the vaguest of ways. Talking the matter over with Charles Oxley—who is Vice President of National VALA—we felt that everything possible should be done to get legislation onto the Statute Book at the earliest possible moment, to ensure that such perverted men should be prohibited from propagating their ideas and behaviour. So working with Mr Geoffrey Dickens, the M.P. for Littleborough and Saddleworth who had attempted to introduce similar legislation in the previous session of Parliament, we compiled a short Bill in the hope that it would be introduced by one of the M.P.s successful in the ballot for Private Member's Bills. In order to make sure that the 'top ten' of the successful Members were given a sight of this Bill at the earliest opportunity, Geoffrey Dickens and I were ready with copies outside the committee room in which the ballot had taken place, immediately Members came out.

On the same day Mr Dickens met with the Home Secretary to urge in the strongest terms that the Government should take action, in case the Bill could not be presented as a Private Member's Bill. Charles Oxley followed this up with his own personal letter to Mr Leon Brittan, and I quote an extract from that letter because it sets out so clearly the sort of information which readers would find very useful in approaching their own Member of Parliament to initiate or support legislation to outlaw PIE.

Over the ten years of the organisation's existence, the leaders have vigorously pursued their aims by publishing a magazine called MAGPIE; by addressing meetings of students at Universities and Colleges; by distributing their literature in homosexual clubs, left-wing political clubs and book shops, and in public libraries. The executive committee of nine members meets monthly to review progress and to plan new ways of promoting adult/child sexual activity. Enclosed are some stickers used in one of their recruitment drives. They give advice to members on ways of seducing children as young as three or four years of age, recommending the practice of hanging around children's playgrounds in public parks and leisure centres, and making friends with families with the object of gaining the parent's confidence to allow them to take children on outings or to allow them to 'baby sit'.

I am aware that there is great reluctance to proscribe an organisation which claims merely to be trying to educate the public and to reform the law, because of the great value of freedom of speech, but there are some essential differences between normal pressure groups and PIE and there are compelling reasons for the proscription of PIE.

The main and crucial difference is that PIE wants to decriminalise a most appalling crime, perpetrated against the most vulnerable members of society, namely small children, exposing them to long-term physical, psychological and emotional harm. The corrupting nature of the harm done is likely to trap the child into continued sexual perversion into adult life, so putting other small children at risk. The sexual abuse of children is worse than rape in several respects, mainly that a child is less likely to recover psychologically.

If two or three hundred men formed themselves into an organisation to campaign for the legalisation of rape, recruiting convicted rapists as life members free of subscriptions, openly publishing propaganda to make rape legally and socially acceptable, publicly denouncing laws forbidding rape, their activities would be such an affront to decency and such a danger to society, that they would have to be stopped. But PIE has been allowed to pursue for ten years aims which are of the same character and to use the same methods as those envisaged above.

As I see it, there is a choice of freedoms here: either the freedom of vicious perverts to propagate their perversions or the freedom of children to play in public parks free from the danger of sexual abuse plus the freedom of parents and grandparents from the fear of such molestation of their children and grandchildren.

Among the compelling reasons for the immediate proscription of PIE is that persons who organise themselves to campaign for the acceptance of adult/child sexual relations represent a serious danger to small children and the Government has a clear duty to protect children against such dangers.

Also, the activities of PIE and similar organisations with the same aims represent a danger to our society, and the Government has a clear duty to protect society from such a corrupting influence and to express the strong disapproval and special abhorrence felt by the public at the prospect of the acceptance of adult/child sexual relations.

Furthermore, if Parliament does *not* proscribe PIE and organisations with its aims, the inaction will be seen as tacit acceptance of PIE's credibility and as a recognition of PIE's cause and it will give great encouragement to other pressure groups who are campaigning for the lowering of the 'age of consent'.

Since the publication of the press reports on the conviction of two of the leading members of PIE on the lesser charges and their acquittal on the more serious charges of incitement, I have been inundated with letters from ordinary decent citizens who are horrified that such an organisation is allowed to exist. Most letters are from mothers and grandmothers.

I have also received several letters and telephone calls from mothers whose children have been sexually abused, but who have not reported the offence for fear of publicity, or fear of reprisal, or because of a lack of faith in the judicial system to punish criminals.

You, Sir, will know how difficult it is to prove incitement to sexual crimes, hence the acquittal of men whom I knew to be guilty of such offences. I sat and listened to members of the executive committee of PIE boasting to one another of their 'successes'.

With great respect, Sir, may I urge you most earnestly to initiate or to give Government support to legislation to proscribe organisations whose aims include the legal and social acceptance of adult sexual relations with children under the age of sixteen years.

Quite how far we are likely to get at this time with legislation[1] to protect our children against the threat of paedophilia is uncertain. I personally feel—and may I be proved wrong as soon as possible—that the country as a whole and therefore Parliament itself is not yet ready for a wholesale attack upon it, but that is reason why all those who care—and that is surely everyone—about the health and happiness of children should not first face the problem and determine to do everything possible to deal with it, however great our own sense of repugnance may be.

The truth is, of course, that until quite recently the subject of child sex abuse has been virtually taboo, though recent research shows that it has always been a reality in the lives of far more children than we have been prepared even to talk about. And of course the child who is sexually abused by a father or mother (experience shows that while it is usually the father who is physically involved with the child, the mother often colludes with silence out of fear of the consequences of admitting that she even knows) is so confused and frightened that he or she becomes incapable of knowing what is right or wrong, normal or abnormal.

Charles Oxley in fact was not the only one campaigning against paedophilia. Hungarian-born Gitta Sereny, (whom we have already quoted in chapter 4) worked for some time with displaced children. Her childhood experiences of being separated from her family during the Second World War gave her great sensitivity to, and understanding of, the problems of child prostitution

[1]See Appendix (p.153)

and paedophilia in America, Britain and in Germany. Writing in the *Sunday Times* (November 25th 1984) Gitta Sereny wrote

> If we are to speak of 'children's rights'—one of the Paedophiles' banner cries—then the first right of every child is to be helped to grow in safety, into a happy and useful adult. If our primary purpose is to achieve this goal, then regretfully we may be forced into unwelcome acts of censorship and restrictive laws. We may be forced to back-track on laws and rules which experience has proved to be too liberal, too permissive. Even further we may need laws which would allow and indeed oblige judges to pronounce the most severe sentences—not only equal to but exceeding those handed out every day for burglary or carrying weapons.
>
> What is being 'stolen' from thousands of our children is far worse than any burglary. It is their future.

It seems to me that as caring and compassionate people we have to think of the paedophiles themselves—not as moral lepers beyond our concern, but as real people with real needs. At the time of the paedophile case in 1982 the NSPCC published a statement about its own activities in this field, and very thought-provoking it was. The Society suggested that the old approach of imprisoning adults responsible for child sex abuse— usually the father—can lead to the break up of the family and to the child being placed in care. It pointed out that the child then often feels guilty about being the cause of 'splitting up the family' and especially if he/she was the one who brought the problem out into the open. The Society is therefore now experimenting with counselling and therapy of repentant offenders, and is busy training specialized officers to advise social workers.

Beyond and above this, of course, comes the responsibility of the parents—*all* parents. Are we open enough to talk to our children about their bodies, about their feelings and about sex? Are we sensitive and responsible enough to teach them the rights and wrongs of human relationships—not only from a sexual angle? While it is true that sex is an important aspect of life, it will only find its true role as an expression of the *whole* personality.

We need to face again the role of the media in creating the kind of climate where this type of sad and perverted experience is on the increase in our so-called 'civilized' society. As Gitta Sereny says, 'If we persist in blunting the sensitivities of both children and adults by overt and vulgar sex in stories, photographs and films—without the relief of tenderness, then we are playing our part in corrupting them.' Amen to that.

I realize, as I write, how easy and indeed natural it is to feel overwhelmed by problems such as the one we have been talking about in this chapter. But, as I say to myself time and time again, the burdens such children have to carry are finally a reproach to everyone of us, no matter how free our own children may be from such experiences. We are where we are, and the children are exposed to what they are exposed to, because as a nation we have turned our back upon God. We have to accept that the dark side of man's nature is increasingly given not only sway, but credence, in our common life. The truth is that these suffering children and the shamed and shameful adults who are the cause of their suffering are a product of our unwillingness to declare the truth as we know it, in season and out, and to pay the price for so doing.

Conclusion

It would be very wrong of me to give the impression that there have been no 'sloughs of despond' and that there have not been many times when I have felt utterly lost as I've been faced—and indeed, have sometimes myself created—circumstances quite beyond anything I have ever known before. I have sometimes felt totally out of my depth—agonizingly so—without human understanding or previous experience on which to fall back.

Most vividly, as I write, I am conscious of the strain and challenges which arise when someone with a background such as mine and with no political experience as such finds herself with decisions to make which also involve people at the very heart of Government, whom one has come to know as individuals. How much easier to be a raw nobody, with no understanding of the way in which one's public statements and actions would affect those whom one knew simply by their names and role! The more I have come to know the people behind the official titles, the harder it has often been to challenge them publicly. The spiritual challenge is real and hard. Is it more important to care what such people think of me than to raise, publicly, issues which I feel need to be so raised? Or is it better to work 'behind the scenes'?

And if so, what happens not only to the mobilization of public concern, but also to the whole process of informing the public of what is going on—thus, hopefully, giving those who wish to fight the ammunition with which to do so?

All this could be the raw material of depression and impotence. What is more, there are no human answers to the anxiety of upsetting people whom one very deeply respects, to the fear that doors which were welcomingly open will close. One has to 'let go' and seek an answer where only the answers are to be found—in the Word of God himself.

It was during one of these times of feeling that 'everything's too much', and I was tempted to turn my back on it all, that I took my Bible and quietly but intensely prayed that the Lord would give me 'a word' when I opened it. So he did—I began to read the third chapter of Malachi, and my eyes fell on verse 10:

> 'Test me in this' says the Lord Almighty 'and see if I will not throw open the floodgates of heaven and pour out so much blessing that you will not have room enough for it.' (NIV)

So much that characterizes our life, and particularly our culture, eats away the essence not only of human dignity but of what it means to be a child of God. This is why I return constantly to the danger implicit in comforting ourselves with the idea that somehow, if we busy ourselves with 'good works', others will somehow solve the problem for us. Or, more dangerous still, that they will go away—'What the eye doesn't see the heart will not grieve over.' It may not, but the price will be paid by someone, somewhere, and it will be a far greater price because of our spiritual complacency. Hard words? Preachifying? What right have I?

Of one thing I am sure. We are called into dangerous ways. Each one of us must pray constantly—not in any routine or academic fashion—not only for courage and for guidance but also for a continuing sense of God's reassurance.

We must pray to be shockproof, yet shockable; to keep our sensitivity but not carry burdens in our own strength. We must pray that the Lord will take care of our mind and spirit.

We must pray that we will know what it is to be utterly exhausted, yet have faith; and to claim the strength and spirit to keep going.

There is a convincing historical argument that Britain was saved from a revolution similar to that which swept France because of the teaching of John Wesley and the spread of the Evangelical Revival. In our days of comfort and self-concern it's worth recalling that the average age at which evangelists died in the days of John Wesley was thirty-two. Not, of course, that the social and medical conditions of those days can be compared with ours; but such a life span was very short even then. They were on fire for Jesus Christ and, it seems to me, that we in our generation also need to be on fire with a determination to respond to the challenge of what it means to be Christian at the end of the twentieth century.

The press release put out by BBC's Radio 4 just before Christmas 1984 was very interesting indeed! It stated that in response to many requests from listeners its programmes would contain more *Christian* biblical content than usual. I was delighted to hear how they put this promise into practice, but perhaps even more delighted—because of its deep significance—to know that this decision had been made because ordinary people had taken the trouble to put pen to paper and the BBC had responded. There is so much to learn from that about the opportunities we have if we'll take them; and there is so much encouragement in the response itself. Could it be that many of the things which disturb and offend us are, to a greater extent than we realize, the product of an accepted interpretation by programme makers of what *we* want? Could it also be that if we all undertook to build up our own personal relationship with those who make the decisions about what we see and hear for so many hours of the day and night, very different standards would emerge? Producers, directors and executives are all people. Many of them have families. Many of them care just as we do. Nevertheless they often spend their working lives in small, self-contained units, in which certain myths about the public at large take root.

That leads to the gradual erosion of the truth about the kind of people the rest of us really are.

* * *

'Keep me, Lord, very close to you that I may be that homely tool on which you can rely and which will not let you down. I look around me and on my writing table I see there humble and reliable tools, with which I write as an extension of my hand; Lord, I would be your hands in action, your reliable tool, as near to you as the sword is to the soldier or the prayer book to the one who holds it.'

Pierre Charles, 'Prayer for all times'

EPILOGUE

'Go to It, Girl!'

I wrote in my diary the morning after I stayed up to watch *Scum* on the 10th June 1983—'What can one say about it except that it was a presentation, from beginning to end, of sadistic violence—it served no useful purpose—no Borstal could be an institution of such totally unrelieved evil.

'Will have to do something, the constant use of the four letter word set a new low for television—if they can get away with this they can get away with anything. Should we consider seeking a judicial declaration that in transmitting it Channel 4 were breaking the law? My feeling is that we should.'

That was how it all began, and I think it's important that I am more specific about the kind of violence which was in the film so that readers can judge for themselves, if they did not see the programme, just how extreme it was. There were, amongst others, scenes of kicking in the genitals, a coshing, using a sock full of billiard balls, an attempted braining of someone with an iron bar, an attempted drowning in a wash basin, and a homosexual rape.

The following morning I discussed the matter with our legal advisor and he came over to view a recording of the film for himself. He had no doubt but that we should indeed go for a judicial declaration and so we did.

We had in fact known about the film *Scum* for several years before it was transmitted on Channel 4. It was first made for the BBC, but its Director General Mr Alasdair Milne refused to allow it to be shown in 1978 in its 'Play for To-day' series, and was courageous enough to come on to the television screen to explain his decision. His decision did, as was only to be expected, cause an outcry from the 'anti-censorship-at-all-costs-lobby'. However Mr Milne stuck to his ground. The film was then shown in the cinema with an 'X' certificate which meant, of course, that no-one under eighteen could see it. However Channel 4 started to take an interest in screening the film. The officer with special responsibility for films at the Independent Broadcasting Authority, remembering the earlier controversy, decided to view the film along with his colleagues on the film committee.

After seeing it they sent a memo to Mr Colin Shaw, then Director of Television at the IBA, which read, 'We have grave doubts about allowing it to be shown. It contains a lot of violence and bad language, but even that could be defensible were it a film of any merit. In our view it is not. It is essentially an exploitation movie with stereotype characters appealing to the baser instincts which we feel would be difficult to defend.'

Such condemnation could not be ignored and so Mr Shaw decided to view the film himself. Having done so, he sent the following memo to Mr John Whitney, the Director General at the IBA: '*Scum* has, in our view, all the signs of having been made in an attempt to exploit the sensation which followed the BBC's decision to ban the television production.'

At that point Mr Whitney decided to look at the film in the privacy of his home where he watched it with his wife. This, he felt, would enable him to judge the film in the kind of setting in which viewers would view it. Mr Whitney was, in fact, a trustee of a prisoners' Self Help group, and felt this gave him some 'inside' understanding of such institutions. He said later that *Scum* was in his view 'a serious dramatic work based in the tensions and violence that are a feature of a closed prison society'. He felt that it was 'a film of merit which deserved to be shown'. So it was shown.

It has to be said that the evidence of support for Mr Whitney's view is very sparse indeed. Typical of the response to the film was a letter in the *Birmingham Post* from a Mr michael Kelly, a prison officer, who said that *Scum* was a gross insult to all the caring staff—officers and civilians—who work in such difficult establishments and who, contrary to sections of the media, do such professional work with boys and girls aged between 15 and 21.'

He went on:

> Violence and bullying, if evident, is quickly stamped out and strict codes of behaviour exist via the Prison Rule 47 discipline report procedure.
>
> Each establishment is answerable to its own Board of Visitors, who are laymen and women who act as public watchdogs and have great influence within an establishment. If necessary, they can suspend on recommendation any member of staff.
>
> This disgusting film, which apparently had already been censored, plummeted Channel 4 to an all-time low in standards of decency and honesty.
>
> Obviously we do handle inmates who are, by their lifestyle, inveterately violent. They are professionally dealt with on behalf of society and ostracised from others via

Prison Rule 43, until they can accept conformity of regulations with acceptable behaviour patterns.

We are accountable to the public and I hope that this letter will act as reassurance after the damage done by this irresponsible film.

Our application for a judicial declaration was finally heard in the High Court on April 13th 1984 and Lord Justice Watkins declared that 'having regard to the IBA's statutory duties and to the history of divergent opinion as to the propriety of the film *Scum*, the Director General committed a grave error of judgment in failing to refer it to the IBA for its decision as to whether it be shown'. He concluded his declaration by saying that I, as a licence holder, had 'sufficient interest to entitle her to seek and to obtain relief by way of declaration.... I grant it, as I have already indicated, because I feel it is outstandingly important that so powerful a thing in our lives as television be carefully controlled.' His Lordship went further, saying that the Independent Broadcasting Authority itself was 'in breach of its duties' in not instructing the Director General in what circumstances he should refer a programme to the Authority before it was shown. And I was granted costs.

I was, of course, delighted by the result, feeling that it not only vindicated the action we'd taken but also because I felt it had underlined the rights of the ordinary citizen when faced with the power of a mighty Authority. The case would also, I felt, have a great impact on television standards in the future because the IBA would have to exert its authority more.

However the IBA decided—I'm told reluctantly!—to go to Appeal and that was heard on 3rd April 1985. What long drawn out affairs legal cases are! In the event the Appeal Court Judges, one of whom was Lord Donaldson, Master of the Rolls—Lord Denning's successor—cleared the IBA and rejected as 'misplaced' the criticisms made by the High Court Judges of Mr John Whitney and of the IBA. They said that the Authority's monitoring system, aimed at ensuring that programmes did not offend against good taste and decency, was not unreasonable, and the IBA was granted costs estimated at £30,000.

On the day of the judgement we had been up at 5.30 am—having gone into London the day before—and by midday, after the announcement in the High Court, all the press and radio interviews, as well as a conference with my counsel and solicitor, Ernest and I were more than ready to go home. We took a taxi to Liverpool Street Station arriving with just two minutes to spare and flung ourselves into our seats in a state of almost total exhaustion.

No sooner had we done so than the guard's voice came booming out of the tannoy. 'If Mrs Mary Whitehouse is on the train would she please report to the enquiry office on platform 9.' We looked at one another in amazement and I left everything and rushed out of the carriage. The guard said he'd hold up the train while I rang the telephone number I was given. It was to ITV's 'News at One'—would I come on to the programme? It was by that time already 12.35 pm and the first thought that came into my mind was that I couldn't possibly start again—after all, I'd already had seven packed and pretty intense hours! But suddenly, a voice, so strong and insistent said to me, incredibly, 'Go to it, girl! Go to it!'

So I went. I was asked by presenter Leonard Parkin what I proposed to do next, and I told him what had been decided earlier that morning, namely that we would petition the House of Lords for leave to appeal to that House. 'We shall go all the way,' I said cheerfully!

When I was asked whether I would be able to find the £30,000 I said that, of course, I did not have the money, 'but that right from the beginning of our campaign we have had to make decisions which we have felt have been right without saying "Is the money there?" first. Throughout it all we have trusted and, in one way or another, it has come out right in the end.'

And indeed it did! Later that day I had a phone call asking me next morning to ring a particular telephone number and ask for a certain director of Deloittes, Haskins and Sell, one of the very top City accountants.

I did so and was told that one of their clients had seen me on 'News at One' and wanted to pay the costs for me! What an amazing and wonderful experience that was, and I never cease to wonder at it. If I had failed to obey the prompting and followed my surely perfectly justified sense that I'd already done as much as I possibly could, it would never have happened!

And I have to say too, that there were many more phone calls and letters with offers of financial help and, indeed, gifts continued to flow in even after. On Easter Sunday, just three days after the hearing, the newspapers carried the news that my costs had been covered.

Now, as I write, we await the outcome of our Petition to the House of Lords for the right to appeal further. How can I say otherwise than that I believe it is all in the Lord's hands? If I am ever tempted to doubt that, I recall the way in which he used so wonderfully the laying of the costs of the case to my empty hands. Very humbly I realize that my cheerful faith that all would be well, which many millions saw on more than one news bulletin, was fully vindicated. What a practical witness to his power, caring and involvement!

APPENDIX 1

The British Humanist Association

The British Humanist Association is a comparatively new association, formed from a number of ethical, humanist and secularist groups, and as such dates from 1963. Its formation began a new era in humanism because it is highly organized, centralized and influential, despite its small membership. It operates from one room at 13, Prince of Wales Terrace and has about 60 local groups.[1] Its total membership in 1970 was 4,100 and less than 2,000 by 1978, but its influence is as strong as ever.

It is affiliated to the International Humanist and Ethical Union formed in 1951, which is particularly active in Europe, again despite its small membership. The IHEU has consultative status with UNESCO.

The National Secular Society appears to have its origins in the 1860s, but it had little impact on public opinion until about ten years ago. Its membership in 1970 was about 2,300 but it has since declined.

Brief Summary of Humanist 'Beliefs'

These are quoted from the British Humanist Association's pamphlet *Humanism and the BHA*. They appear in various forms in other BHA publications.

[1]Directory of British Associations.

We do not believe in God.

We accept nothing as revealed truth, not the ten commandments or the theories of Marx or Freud.

We do not believe there is any 'ultimate purpose' to life.

We find the idea of life after death a monumental piece of wishful thinking.

On morals, they say, 'We believe those actions which lead to human happiness are good and those which lead to human unhappiness are bad.' They also believe that whatever the majority thinks to be good *is* good just because it thinks so, and that morality therefore concerns itself with the standards which people from time to time are prepared to accept, not what they ought to accept.

The BHA organizes lobbying campaigns: their members and groups all over the country write to their M.P.s and to the provincial and national newspapers. This is designed to give the impression that there is a nationwide demand for what they advocate. They closely scrutinise denominational newspapers and periodicals, and this gives them information which enables them to exploit the differences of opinion among the Christian churches.

They try to influence one M.P. to introduce in Parliament a Bill embodying one of their particular aims (as they did with David Steel and his Abortion Bill in 1967). For this purpose they hold in readiness 'model' Parliamentary Bills (e.g. on Euthanasia) or amendments to existing Acts (e.g. on Religious Education).

They campaign against all attempts to introduce legislation designed to remedy the abuses of the laws which they themselves helped to put on the Statute book (e.g. measures intended to amend the 1967 Abortion Act).

The humanist M.P.s form the Humanist Parliamentary Group, and also seek to draw to themselves those M.P.s who are not committed to any church or religious organization.

Infiltration and representation: They get themselves elected to the committees of organizations likely to be useful in furthering humanist aims: e.g. the Religious Education Council, and the Social Morality Council. They are active in gaining wide humanist representation throughout the country on local Standing Advisory Councils for Religious Education (SACRE).

Affiliation: Here one cannot do better than quote from the BHA annual report for 1977: 'Whilst we cannot match the financial and manpower resources of the churches, we can through the enthusiasm of each and every individual member greatly extend our influence and activities....' The report goes on to say that the BHA is 'represented on, and takes an active interest in, the work of other bodies including the United Nations Association, the Co-ordinating Committee in Defence of the 1967 Abortion Act, the Religious Education Council of England and Wales, the National Council for Civil Liberties and the National Peace Council. Members of the Association serve, in an individual capacity, on the Committees of the Social Morality Council and of the Charity Law Reform Committee.' The BHA has already made a submission to the United Nations to remove from parents the right to bring up their own children according to their conscience, in their own beliefs.

The BHA advocates and promotes legislation on the following:[1]

   a) Euthanasia.
   b) Easier divorce.
   c) Abolition of all forms of censorship.
   d) Repeal of the laws against blasphemy and obscenity.
   e) Abolition of the present legal 'age of consent' and the removal of penalties for incest.
   f) Repeal of legislation giving tax and rate reliefs to religious organizations.
   g) Repeal of the adoption laws in so far as they safeguard the natural mother's choice of religion for her child.
   h) Legalization of the use of so-called 'soft drugs'.
   i) Repeal of all legislative and social measures against homosexuality.

[1] Quoted from *Humanism and Secularism in England and Wales*, published by the Catholic Teachers' Federation.

BBC and ITV telephone numbers and addresses

Addresses:	Phone Numbers:

BBC

BBC, London, W1A 1AA (Radio)	01-580 4468
BBC TV Centre, London, W12 7RJ	01-743 8000
BBC, Glasgow, G12 8DG	041-339 8844
BBC, Cardiff, CF5 2YQ	0222-564888
BBC, Belfast, BT2 8HQ	0232 244400
BBC East, Norwich, NR1 3ND	0603 28841
BBC Midlands, Birmingham, B5 7QQ	021-472 5353
BBC North, Leeds, LS2 9PX	0532 41181
BBC North East, Newcastle Upon Tyne, NE1 8AA	0632 320961
BBC North West, Manchester, M60 1SJ	061-236 8444
BBC South, Southampton, SO9 1PF	0703 26201
BBC South West, Plymouth, PL3 5BD	0752 29201
BBC West, Bristol BS8 2LR	0272 732211

ITV Companies

Independent Broadcasting Authority, London, SW3 1EY	01-584 7011
Anglia TV, Norwich, NR1 3JG	0603 615151
Border TV, Carlisle, CA1 3NT	0228 25101
Central TV, Birmingham, B1 2JP	021-643 9898
Channel Four, London, W1P 2AX	01-631 4444

Channel TV, Jersey, C.I.	0534 73999
Grampian TV, Aberdeen, AB9 2XJ	0224 646464
Granada TV, Manchester, M60 9EA	061-832 7211
HTV, Cardiff, CF1 9XL	0222 590590
ITN, London, W1P 4DE	01-637 2424
London Weekend TV, London, SE1 9LT	01-261 3434
Scottish TV, Glasgow, G2 3PR	041-332 9999
Thames TV, London, NW1 3BB	01-387 9494
Television South, Southampton, SO9 5HZ	0703 34211
Television South West, Plymouth, PL1 2SP	0752 663322
TV-AM, London, NW1 8EF	01-267 4300
Tyne Tees TV, Newcastle Upon Tyne, NE1 2AL	0632 610181
Ulster TV, Belfast, BT7 1EB	0232 228122
Yorkshire TV, Leeds, LS3 1JS	0532 438283

'EVIL TRIUMPHS WHEN GOOD MEN DO NOTHING'

The country gets the broadcasting it deserves—TV and radio standards depend upon you.

The pen (and the phone) are mightier than the sword.

Use the addresses and telephone numbers listed above to **make your voice heard**.

When telephoning ask to speak to the Duty Officer, who will note your complaint.

Copies of these details can be obtained from:

>   Mrs Mary Whitehouse, CBE,
>   Ardleigh,
>   COLCHESTER,
>   Essex, CO7 7RH.

When writing to the BBC or to ITV and Channel 4, always do so in specific terms.

a) Address your letter, not to 'The BBC' or to 'Granada TV' for example, but to the producer of the programme—the name will certainly be in *Radio Times* or *TV Times*, and is sometimes in the press TV guides.

b) Be specific about what has pleased or offended you. Give details of language or behaviour. When appropriate quote from the various codes published by both BBC and ITV.

Just how effective such action can be is reflected in a series of letters which passed between one of our members, his M.P., and the BBC.

Angered by foul language in a Radio 4 programme broadcast at 6.30 pm the person concerned wrote first to the BBC; but when he did not receive a reply he wrote to his M.P., who then wrote to the Chairman of the BBC, Mr Stuart Young. In his reply to the M.P. Mr Young stated that the matter of bad language had been discussed by Mr David Hatch, Controller of Radio 4, with Light Entertainment producers 'and they will have to ensure that no bad language of the kind objected to will be heard in the 6.30 programmes on Radio 4.' The M.P. forwarded the letter to our member who then wrote to Mr Young to say how grateful he was for the action taken by Mr Hatch. He added 'Having listened to the programme over the last three weeks, I am pleased to report that *no* bad language has been used or intimated.' One can only add—it just goes to show how effective such exercises can be!

c) Keep a copy of your letter.

d) If you receive only a card of acknowledgement or are dissatisfied by the reply write either to Mr Alasdair Milne, the Director General of the BBC, or to Mr John Whitney, the Director General of the IBA.

e) If you still do not get satisfaction send the copy of your letter to your M.P.—if you do not know his name, address it, M.P. for, and name of your town. That will be quite adequate. Tell him you find the reply unsatisfactory and ask him/her to take up the matter on your behalf. Such a step always produces a considered and even apologetic response.

f) Do take notes on which you can base your letter as soon as the programme is finished—if you wait till the morning you will very likely have forgotten exactly what happened.

APPENDIX 3

Video Recordings Act

Mr Graham Bright's Bill gave to an authority 'to be designated by the Home Office' the task of classifying videos. The authority will be the British Board of Film Censors. Classification involves labelling the films as suitable for viewing by persons above or under a certain age: the age demarcations are expected to be the same as the existing BBFC cinema classifications of UC (especially suitable for children), U, PG (Parental Guidance), 15, 18 and 18 R. The Board will take into account suitability for 'viewing in the home'. The most contentious area covers 18 R videos. It is anticipated that this classification will cover soft porn and semi-hard porn, while hard porn and video nasties will be unclassified and unavailable. No one knows where the margins lie.

There will be exemptions from the classifications process. The Bill will exempt works designed 'to inform, educate, or instruct', works concerned with sport, religion or music, and video games. However the exemption does not apply if the work depicts 'human sexual activity or acts of force or restraint associated with such activity'; or 'mutilation or torture of, or other acts of gross violence towards humans or animals'; or 'human genital organs or human urinary or excretory functions'. The cost of classification will be borne by the video maker and is likely, on average, to be something in the region of £400–£600.

APPENDIX 4

The NVALA's comments upon The Home Office Committee on Obscenity and Film Censorship

(Chaired by Professor Bernard Williams, 1979)

The Committee concluded that the present laws relating to obscenity and film censorship were 'a mess' (paragraph 2.29) and recommended that they should be scrapped and replaced by a comprehensive new statute (paragraph 13.4.1).

It argued that terms such as 'obscene', 'indecent' and 'deprave and corrupt', used in the present laws, were no longer useful and recommended that they should be abandoned entirely.

However, while agreeing that the present laws need amendment, National VALA disagrees with the claim by the Committee that the words 'obscene' and 'indecent' are no longer useful, but agrees that the term 'deprave and corrupt', as used in the present law, creates problems.

National VALA felt the Committee's recommendations that hard core pornography, including even bestiality, should be made available in 'restricted' shops i.e. sex shops was, to say the least, extraordinarily unimaginative and almost unbelievably naive. Such a recommendation may control points of sale but in no way its circulation. One is bound to ask whether the Committee discussed the eventuality of such material, once bought, being passed around and left about in every kind of circumstance.

National VALA disagreed entirely with the Committee's

proposal to remove all legal controls over printed obscenity, and it was convinced and said so that its implementation would have a disastrous effect upon British culture, education, broadcasting, etc.

The Williams Report, though debated in Parliament was never voted upon. Nevertheless some of the recommendations made by the Report have been surreptitiously incorporated into common practice such as the licensing of sex shops to which National VALA was totally opposed as we felt it gave them an aura of legitimacy and acceptability.

Local Government (Miscellaneous Provisions) Act 1982

This Act introduces licensing requirements in respect of 'Sex Shops' and 'Sex Cinemas'. The provisions have to be adopted by the Council before they can be brought into force. (NB The provisions relating to Sex Cinemas cannot be brought into force until a day to be appointed by the Secretary of State.)

Applications for licences

If the Council adopts the provisions no premises, vehicle, vessel, or stall may be used as a sex establishment except with a licence unless a waiver has been granted. Applicants have to give public notice of their application by advertisement in a local newspaper and by displaying a notice on or near the premises which are the subject of the application. Such notice has to be displayed for 21 days in a place where it can conveniently be read by the public.

The applicant also has to send a copy of his application to the Chief Officer of Police. An applicant who knowingly makes a false statement in his application will be guilty of an offence for which the maximum penalty is a fine of £10,000.

Existing premises

Where a person who was using premises as a sex establishment, immediately before the first publication in a newspaper of the Council's decision to bring the provisions into force, applies for a licence before the date appointed for the coming into force of the provisions it will be lawful for him to continue so to use the premises pending the determination of the application. All applications made before the date upon which the provisions are brought into force have to be considered before any single application is determined and preference has to be given to applicants who are using premises as a sex establishment and were so using them on 22 December 1981 or who are successors of such persons.

Objections

Any member of the public may object to the grant of a licence by writing to the Council within 28 days of the application. The Council has to give the applicant written notice of the general terms of any objection but must not reveal the identity of the objector unless he agrees.

Determination of applications

Before granting a licence (which will last for a period not exceeding one year) the Council must have regard to any observations made by the Police and to any written objections that have been made. Before an application is refused the applicant has to be given an opportunity of appearing before and being heard by a Committee or Sub Committee of the Council. The Council has a discretion to refuse an application; if the applicant is unsuitable by reason of having been convicted of an offence or for any other reason; if the business would be managed or carried on for the benefit of a person other than the applicant who would himself be refused a licence; if the number of sex establishments is equal to or exceeds the number which the Council considers is appropriate for the locality, where the premises are situated (Nil may be an appropriate number); or if a licence would be inappropriate having regard to the character of the locality, the use to which any premises in the locality are put, or the layout, character or condition of the premises the subject of the application.

APPENDIX 6

Monitoring

For reference:

The impact of broadcasting on society is such that its output calls for very careful scrutiny. Throughout the western world there is widespread concern about the level and cause of social violence, and there is now much reliable research which demonstrates a clear connection between televised violence and social violence. Furthermore television is increasingly recognized as the contributory factor to social violence which is most easily remedied.

> One hundred and forty-six articles in behavioural science journals, representing 50 studies involving 10,000 children and adolescents from every conceivable background, all showed that violence produces increased aggressive behaviour in the young and that immediate remedial action in terms of television programming is warranted. Four major issues are covered: effects on learning, emotional effects, the question of catharsis and effects on aggressive behaviour.
>
> *The Journal of the American Medical*
> *Association 1975*

> We believe that, while increased exploitation and depiction of violence in the media is only one of the many social factors contributing to crime, it is the largest single variable most amenable to rectification.
>
> *The Royal Commission on Violence—*
> *the Communications Industry* (Ottawa, 1976)

Monitoring television and radio is a vitally important part of National VALA's work. Without reliable information it is impossible for us, as a responsible and respected association, to respond appropriately to programme content.

The main purpose of monitoring is to examine how broadcasting standards measure up to obligations as set out in the Television Act 1956. Broadcasters are in duty bound to ensure that programmes as far as possible do not:

1) Offend against good taste and decency;
2) Offend against public feeling;
3) Incite to crime and disorder;
4) Take sides on matters of public interest.

National VALA reports on various aspects of programme content. Such reports are wholly dependent upon the monitoring activities of our members. To add weight to our representations to the Broadcasters, the Home Secretary or other Members of Parliament, it is essential to have factual evidence.

When monitoring, always take note of date, title of programme, time of transmission and TV channel or radio station. In the case of ITV take note of the companies advertising at the beginning, during, and at the end of the programme. Is the programme British or imported?

Monitoring acts of violence

Which characters use violence? Are they 'good', e.g. policemen, or 'bad', e.g. criminals?

Is the violence explicit, i.e. on screen? or implicit, off screen? Did the camera linger 'on the horror of the blinded face or the severed hand'?

Were any special effects, audio and/or visual, used to emphasise violent acts? For example, were the acts of violence shown in close-up? In slow motion? Accentuated by musical or other effects?

Was the violence (1) gratuitous; (2) sadistic; (3) used against a woman or child or a domestic animal; (4) in a modern or historical setting; (5) within the family?

Look out for domestic utensils used as weapons; take particular note of violence used in a domestic environment.

N.B. 'The violence of the events should never be sensationalized and should always be put into the perspective of the rest of the world's news of the day. Dead bodies should not be shown in close-up and film should not dwell on close-up pictures of the grief-stricken and suffering in the wake of natural disasters or man-made violence.'

Monitoring bad language and blasphemy

List the words or phrases—in their context if possible. Indicate who says the words and to whom. In the context of the programme were these 'good' characters or 'bad'? Indicate the circumstances, e.g. in the house, in the presence of women or children, in a public place.

Monitoring the consumption of alcohol

What is the age of the people involved? Male or female?

Which characters drink and how much—a little, regularly, excessively, obsessively?

Are they 'good' characters—e.g. parents, teachers, clergy, police officers, people in responsible positions or characters with whom young people identify? Or 'bad' characters— feckless and irresponsible people?

Does drinking take place at home or at work or in a public place?

Is it relevant to the story?

Is it a 'social' drink or a resort at a time of tension or unhappiness?

Any drinking before characters drive?

Are spirits or beer drunk?

ITV—Take note of any advertisement for drink giving time, date and name of programme in which it is shown.

Monitoring of sexual themes

How explicit is the sexual content?
Is sex used simply to bolster a weak plot?
What age of characters are involved?
Was the sex promiscuous and/or outside marriage?
Was it in close-up and did it turn viewers into voyeurs?
Was any cruelty involved?

*Extracts from 'The Portrayal of Violence in Television Programmes—
A Note of Guidance' (BBC, 1972 republished in 1979 in a combined
report with the IBA.*

The fact that most people in Britain rarely encounter direct
violence of a physical kind lays a particular obligation on
television to be truthful in its reflection of violence.... 'It
must neither stir up unnecessary anxieties nor lead people to
believe that physical violence is a readily acceptable solution
to problems and conflicts.

Section 4

It should be recognised that children watching in the late
evening are, in some cases, less likely to be subject to adequate
supervision. The BBC cannot accept an exclusive responsibility towards these children...but nevertheless producers
should have regard to their presence and therefore to the
need for portraying violence in programmes only when
warranted and then only to the degree justified. The basic
criterion must be whether the use of violence is likely to
sharpen or to blunt the human sensitivities of the viewer.

Section 5 Children and violence

It follows that he [the producer] must include violence in his
programmes only after the most careful consideration of his
motives for doing so. Among the factors he must consider are
these—

(a) ...Adults may regard plays depicting family insecurity
and marital infidelity as commonplace, but such plays
may be, in certain forms, deeply disturbing to children.

(b) ...Children are likely to be particularly disturbed by

violence in a setting which closely resembles their own. Thus, an incident in which someone who looks like a child's father strikes someone who looks like its mother is probably very disturbing, threatening as it does the child's sense of security in the home.

(c) Small children in particular work in much shorter dimensions of time than adults. Tomorrow is a long way off, next week an eternity away. In story-telling programmes, drama serials, or feature films divided into several episodes, the dramatic effect of violent 'cliff-hangers' at the end of individual instalments should be treated with caution. Young children often regard each instalment as complete in itself and may not be able to see or may even avoid seeing subsequent episodes which could provide the resolution of the situation. For young children even a week may be too long to wait for reassurance that the characters with whom they identify are safe. If regular and well-loved presenters of factual children's programmes are involved in violent situations, care must be taken to show that they are safe and well afterwards.

(d) The loyalties of young children are simple. They will commit themselves to one side in a conflict, content to accept a black-and-white resolution and not considering the possibilities of alternative solutions. This means that shades of 'goodness' and 'badness' in characters have to be treated with great care.

(e) It is particularly important that 'good' characters should not perform actions which might appear cruel to the child audience, however honourable the intentions of the 'good' characters may be. There is some evidence that children more readily copy the 'bad' actions of good characters than those of bad characters.

(f) Although instances of the imitation of harmful behaviour are rare, it is commonsense to avoid setting examples which can easily be copied: such as the use of knives or broken bottles in fights, nooses, trip-wires, karate chops, or the locking-up of 'prisoners' in outhouses, empty rooms, or cellars. While guns, being less accessible, and fists, being less harmful, might seem open to less objection on these grounds, the latter can be more readily resorted to by children and therefore provide an easier example for imitation. The details of manufacture of weapons should not be given, especially when the materials may be close at hand; for example, in the case of nail-bombs and molotov-cocktails. For the same reasons, care should be taken in choosing the risks to which characters are exposed, so that children are not encouraged to seek out the same hazards for themselves.

(g) Violence as an inevitable solution to a fictional situation should only be invoked in relatively rare instances; particularly it is to be avoided in contexts which relate to the child's own life.

(h) The details of fights should not be dwelt upon. However, the impression should not be given that a man can be struck, without danger, on the head. Despite the conventions of saloon punch-ups in Westerns, the head is a very vulnerable part of the body and children should not be encouraged to regard it as an acceptable target.

Section 7 Young people and violence

…the prime danger may be thought to lie in the provision of an inadequate range of stereotypes with which the young people can choose to identify. A variety of images should be available and any attempt to make violence an essential characteristic of manliness, for example, should be avoided.

Section 8 The adult audience and violence

(i) *Programmes other than News or Current Affairs*

…A sequence involving violence must arise naturally from the story and not be used simply to bolster a flagging plot or give an added dimension to a slender characterisation. Moreover, even when violence forms a legitimate element in a production, the manner in which it is presented must be carefully thought about. To what extent, for example, is it necessary to see in close-up the

wounds of Caesar? Is a genuinely new dramatic point
made by zooming-in on Oedipus' blind eyes?

(a) Generally speaking the details of the violence should
be avoided...

(b) The object of violence should be considered carefully. By and large, violence towards defenceless
objects is more disturbing than violence towards,
for example, the man who can defend himself.

(c) In programmes for adult audiences, no less care
should be taken than in children's programmes to
avoid providing examples of weapons ready to hand
or of tactics to use in fist fights. Violence ought not
to be presented in ways which might glorify it or
portray it as a proper solution to inter-personal
conflicts.

(ii) *News and Current Affairs Programmes*

The natural and man-made violence which occurs
throughout the world is generally available at high speed
to the world's newsrooms.... It should be kept in mind
that violence seldom occurs without cause and that,
whenever possible, the viewer is owed an explanation of
the violence he is shown.

BBC Produced Drama

...But makers of action/adventure series and of single plays
need to remember that violence is subject to the law of
diminishing returns. Excessive violence may rob the audience
of its capacity to concentrate on anything else in the programme either at the time of its use or later. Any competition
between directors in the use of violence for effect could
eventually result in its dramatic point being lost. 'To go one
better' may produce the opposite effect. The recent clamp-
down in the United States on the portrayal of violence affect-
ing human beings has led to the injection of action and
excitement through destruction of property. Cars are no
longer just driven over cliffs; they are seen to fall on rocks and
burst into flames. The effect of this 'hardware violence' can

add to the visual images of violence paraded before the viewer—and to the assault on the ears of screeching brakes and crunching metal. It is merely a substitute for direct man to man violence and such acts of violence should not be introduced to compensate for a lack of quality in the writing. A sequence involving violence must arise naturally from the story and not be used simply to bolster a flagging plot or give an added dimension to slender characterisation.

The ITV Code October 1971

All concerned in the planning, production and scheduling of television programmes must keep in mind the following considerations:

The Content of the programme schedule as a whole

(a) People seldom view just one programme. An acceptable minimum of violence in each individual programme may add up to an intolerable level over a period.

(b) The time of screening of each programme is important. Adults may be expected to tolerate more than children can. The ITV policy of 'family viewing time' until 9 pm entails special concern for younger viewers.

The Ends and the Means

(c) There is no evidence that the portrayal of violence for good or 'legitimate' ends is likely to be less harmful to the individual or to society, than the portrayal of violence for evil ends.

Presentation

(d) There is no evidence that 'sanitized' or 'conventional' violence, in which the consequences are concealed, minimized or presented in a ritualistic way, is innocuous. It may be just as dangerous to society to conceal the results of violence or to minimize them as to let people see clearly the full consequences of violent behaviour, however gruesome: what may be better for society may

be emotionally more upsetting or more offensive for the
individual viewer.

(e)   Violence which is shown as happening long ago or far
away may seem to have less impact on the viewer, but it
remains violence. Horror in costume remains horror.

(f)   Dramatic truth may occasionally demand the portrayal
of a sadistic character, but there can be no defence of
violence shown solely for its own sake, or of the gratuitous
exploitation of sadistic or other perverted practices.

(g)   Ingenious and unfamiliar methods of inflicting pain or
injury—particularly if capable of easy imitation—should
not be shown without the most careful consideration.

(h)   Violence has always been and still is widespread
throughout the world, so violent scenes in news and
current affairs programmes are inevitable. But the editor
or producer must be sure that the degree of violence
shown is essential to the integrity and completeness of
his programme.

The Young and the Vulnerable

(i)   Scenes which may unsettle young children need special
care. Insecurity is less tolerable for a child—particularly
an emotionally unstable child—than for a mature adult.
Violence, menace, and threats can take many forms—
emotional, physical and verbal. Scenes of domestic friction, whether or not accompanied by physical violence,
can easily cause fear and insecurity.

(j)   Research evidence shows that the socially or emotionally
insecure individual, particularly if adolescent, is
specially vulnerable. There is also evidence that such
people tend to be more dependent on television than
others. Imagination, creativity or realism on television
cannot be constrained to such an extent that the legitimate service of the majority is always subordinated to
the limitations of a minority. But a civilized society pays
special attention to its weaker members.

This Code cannot provide universal rules. The programme
maker must carry responsibility for his own decisions. In so

sensitive an area risks require special justification. *If in doubt, cut.* [Our emphasis.]

APPENDIX 7

Paedophile Information Exchange

[What follows is as quoted in the original PIE leaflet]:

PIE was founded in October 1974 by three members of the Scottish Minorities Group who felt that there was a need in Britain for a group for those men and women who were sexually and otherwise attracted to young people below the age of about seventeen. Until March 1975 PIE's sole function is the production of a newsletter; in March it is hoped that an organization will be set up by subscribers and that that organization will undertake the following aims:

1: to clear away, where possible, the myths connected with paedophilia (see below) by various means, including the making public of scientific, sociological and similar information.
2: to give advice and counsel to those isolated or lonely because of their paedophile orientation.
3: to help those in legal difficulties concerning sexual acts with under-age partners that took place with the latter's consent.
4: to campaign, as members see fit, for the legal and social acceptance of paedophile love.
5: to provide a means whereby paedophiles might get in contact with each other.

Paedophilia for the purposes of PIE was defined as 'the sexual or intellectual or emotional (or any combination of these three) relationship between an unrelated sexually mature person and a sexually immature child or maturing adolescent', but there was at least one disagreement to including the word 'unrelated', since it has been argued that some paedophile relationships are incestuous. Apart from that uncertainty, that is PIE's definition; a paedophile is the older partner in such a relationship.

However, most paedophiles who have contacted PIE are adult men who are attracted towards boys between the ages of eight to sixteen, and it seems likely that PIE will develop with a bias in favour of this group, although hopefully without discriminating against other paedophiles.

PROPOSED PAEDOPHILIA (PROTECTION OF CHILDREN) BILL

To be brought to attention of M.P.s, please(!)

1) To make illegal membership of any organization, which supports, encourages, condones or entices adults to have sexual relationships with children.
2) To make it an offence for the members of any such body, or for any individual whether a member of such a body or not to distribute, produce, sell, solicit or advertise any material whether written, printed, photographed or electronically reproduced which advocates in any way sexual relationships between adults and children.

APPENDIX 8

The Post Office Act, 1953

Section 11 of the Post Office Act 1953 prohibits the sending by post of certain articles including 'any indecent or obscene print, painting, photograph, lithograph, engraving, cinematograph film, book, card or written communication, or any indecent or obscene article...' The offence may be tried in the magistrates court or the Crown Court. If a person is convicted on indictment in the Crown Court, he is liable to imprisonment for a term not exceeding twelve months.

Information and Advice on Objecting to the Granting of Sex Shop Licences

Issued by Charles Oxley, Tower College, Rainhill, Merseyside L35 6NE (Telephone: 051–426 4333) from whom further copies may be obtained on receipt of a stamped addressed envelope.

1. Ensure that your local authority has passed a resolution to implement Schedule 3 'Control of Sex Establishments' of the Local Government (Miscellaneous Provisions) Act 1982, by telephoning its Chief Executive Officer.
2. Ascertain from the Chief Executive Officer whether an Application has been made to the local authority for a licence to keep a sex shop. Check with him
   (a) the date of the Application;
   (b) that an advertisement/notice appeared in a local newspaper within seven days of the date of the Application;
   (c) that a notice was displayed on the shop door or window informing the public that an Application has been made and stating the name and address of the person to whom objections should be made.
3. Write at once to the appropriate department of the local authority stating your objection. Your letter should be clearly dated and should refer to a particular Application for a particular shop stating the address of the shop. If the Application is for more than one shop, write a separate letter for each. Your letter, though required to be only 'in general terms', should mention the specific points you

wish to raise at the Hearing. Keep a copy of your letter. Make sure it is received by the appropriate authority within 28 days of the date of the Application, otherwise it will be invalid. Encourage others also to express their objections in writing in their own words.

4. Visit the shop and if you see anything you consider to be indecent (as you will), report to the Police that you have reason to believe that the shop is in breach of the Obscene Publications Act and the Indecent Displays Act. Check whether the Police take any action.

5. Ascertain the date and time and place of the hearing and inform the Chief Executive Officer of your intention to be present and of your wish to make representations at the hearing. You do not need to be a local resident to do so. Encourage others to do likewise.

6. Write to each of your local councillors and encourage others to do so.

7. (a) The Hearing is not a law court and there is no cause for any objector to feel nervous or embarrassed. Do not allow yourself to be intimidated or bamboozled.

(b) A sub-committee of the local Council will hear the application. Prepare your case thoroughly, making your points clearly and concisely. It is much better to avoid reading a 'speech'.

(c) If you know of others who intend to speak at the Hearing, arrange to share the points of objection to avoid undue repetition.

8. Your objections may cover the whole range (see below), but where appropriate the objectors should concentrate on the grounds that a sex shop *'would be inappropriate, having regard to the character of the ... locality'*.

Below is a range of objections which you may like to consider and present to the Hearing.

1. Offence would be caused to all decent people who live or shop in the locality.

2. Pornography is a Degradation of womanhood.

3. Pornography endangers Marriage as it leads to adultery,

the main cause of the breakdown of marriage and divorce.

5. Pornography encourages promiscuity among teenagers, causing venereal disease, unwanted pregnancies, illegitimate births and abortions.

6. Once a pornographic book or magazine leaves the shop, there is no control over it. Some pornographic material will fall into the hands of children.

7. Pornography is addictive and despite protests to the contrary, there is a causal link between pornographic material and sexual assault, rape and murder.

8. A sex shop attracts undesirable persons into the neighbourhood.

9. A sex shop lowers the tone of any locality.

10. Other nearby shop-keepers, parents of children who pass the shop on the way to school and persons who pass the shop on the way to church, to say the least, find such establishments 'inappropriate'.

APPENDIX 10

The Beliefs and Aims of National VALA

National VALA believes

☐ that Christian values are basic to the health and wellbeing of our nation and therefore calls on the broadcasting authorities to reverse the current humanist approach to social, religious and personal issues;

☐ that the Broadcasting Authorities should fulfil their legal obligations to ensure 'that nothing is included in the programmes which offends against good taste or decency or is likely to encourage or incite to crime or lead to disorder or to be offensive to public feeling' and 'that the programmes maintain a proper balance...' (Television Act 1954; Broadcasting Act 1981);

☐ that violence on television contributes significantly to the increase of violence in society and should be curtailed;

☐ that the use of swearing and blasphemy are destructive of our culture and our faith and that the broadcasting authorities are remiss in allowing it;

☐ that sexual innuendo and explicit sex trivialise and cheapen human relationships and undermine marriage and family life;

☐ that the media are indivisible and that the quality of film, theatre and publishing inevitably affects broadcasting standards.

National VALA aims

☐ to encourage viewers and listeners to react effectively to programme content;

☐ to stimulate public and parliamentary discussion on the effects of broadcasting on the individual, the family and society;

☐ to secure effective legislation to control obscenity and pornography in the media—including broadcasting.

Is Life So Dear?

by Brother Andrew

Christians have an enemy, and he doesn't always fight fair. The question is: what does it take to win the fierce spiritual battle that is being fought for men's souls?

Brother Andrew is uncompromising in his call for outright commitment to the gospel. With disturbing clarity he shows how the enemy is within our very gates—not in the shape of communism, or Islam, but our own apathy.

Yet his stories of courage and endeavour will inspire us as we see how God equips his servants to take the gospel into enemy strongholds, no matter where we live or where he sends us.

Kingsway Publications